Crossing the River

Ole Henrik Skjelstad

www.lulu.com

First published by Ole Henrik Skjelstad 10.10.2010

ISBN: 978-1-4466-3529-2

First Edition

All scripture quotations are from the King James Bible of 1611

Because of the dynamic nature of the internet, any Web addresses or links may have changed since publication and may no longer be valid.

Cover art: Jessica Robertson

Cover design: Ole Henrik Skjelstad

Ole Henrik's blog:

www.crossingtheriver.wordpress.com

This book is dedicated to all those who have begun their journey into the mystery

Contents:

Introductions

"As I've taught the message of the Father's grace over the past twenty years, I occasionally meet somebody who seems to be on the fast track in learning and sharing this wonderful message. Ole Henrik Skjelstad is such a person. Through his writings and his presence on the Internet, many people have come to a deeper understanding of just how deep and how wide the agape of the Father really is. Ole Henrik's insights have often caused me to experience one of those moments when a reader thinks about the author's insight, "This had to come to him directly from God's Spirit!" Through his writing I have sometimes found myself thinking about particular aspects of grace in a new and different way than I had ever thought about before.

With the publication of Crossing the River, his ministry will reach many others and, more importantly, the message of the wonderful love and grace of our Father will impact them in a fresh and new way for many. I'm not sure how to describe this book. I would call it a devotional book, but the depth of its content will do more than inspire you as devotional books often do. I would call it a study book but to do so risks the chance that you may think it simply contains doctrinal information.

I think the best way to describe Crossing the River is to call it a photo album. This book depicts the love of the Father, Son and Holy Spirit for us all in a way that may affect you in several ways. There will be moments when you find yourself amazed at the things you learn here. There will be times when you may wipe tears of joy from your eyes. There may be times when you grapple with deeper truth, finding it difficult to believe that our God's love could be that good. But, through it all, you will find yourself seeing Jesus more clearly and simultaneously seeing yourself more clearly.

This will be a book you read more than once. I predict that many people will find a Resting Place as they read it for the first time. I heartily recommend it to you with the confidence that you will see your Father's loving face on these pages."

Steve McVey

"Every time I read the writings of Ole Henrik I am amazed and quickened at the new insights he reveals. Surprises abound from a Scripture or story of lives from the Bible...long-familiar writings to me. There in the midst of the 'known' is a rare...very rare...jewel that shines as though it has been illuminated by a million watt light. I am given yet another wonderful glimpse of the 'diamond' of Christ in His facet named Ole Henrik Skjelstad...joyously adjacent to my facet! I am truly in awe because only a short year ago I did not even know Ole, in addition to the fact that reading is not my passion......but today his writings have become my *much-anticipated delight!*

I believe Ole Henrik is 'a voice of and for our time' to those called to explore the ever-expanding Life of the Father, Son and Holy Spirit and our union with Them leading to the fulfillment of Jesus' final prayer in John 17...*our* ONENESS. Each offering, from Genesis to Revelation, emanates from this ONENESS he has come to know. Ole Henrik's gifts of today will be read by future generations much as we read William Law, Meister Eckhart or Norman Grubb. I believe the writings contained in this book are only the beginning from a pen that cannot be quenched until Ole's living waters have flooded the parched and desperately thirsty body of Christ.

Blessings and revelation to all who read these gems..."

DeeDee Winter

"Ole Henrik is one of those rarest of rare humans whom God has created with such winsome and playfully self-deprecating humor that we are disarmed of our own previous judgments and preconceptions, allowing us to hear God's heart in a fresh, living way. I trust this man, because while he teaches powerful and thoughtful truths, I never feel like I'm listening to an agenda or another spin, but instead the overflow of a heart stunned by the love and grace of God."

John Lynch

"To me, there are three major miracles that we experience in Christ Jesus. These miracles are of far greater glory than any other event which we may consider to be a miracle. They are indeed the greatest miracles of all because they are of an eternal quality, coming from outside the realm of time and space, yet visiting the earth and transfiguring the whole of the material creation into something which has never appeared before.

The first and greatest of these greater than all miracles, which also contains the other two within itself, is truly the greatest miracle in the universe. It is summed up in one word – incarnation. The meaning of incarnation is twofold. The first is familiar to most everyone, because it is used to describe the miracle of how the holy, invisible, transcendent God and Creator of the Universe, the Wholly Other, in the form of the Only Begotten Son, came to earth as a complete and total human being.

Jesus Christ, born of a woman, was as much a man as any man who ever lived. But He was also as much God as God is Eternally God. How that can be is an impenetrable mystery to our reasoning minds: indeed, it can make no sense and surpasses all human reason. And yet He came as a babe, as we all do. Then He grew up as any other human being, in all appearances so normal a human being that when He first announced Who He really was to the people in Nazareth who had known Him for most of His thirty years, it drove them to a fierce rage. To them He was a man like any other, not different from them in any discernable way, and it was blasphemy of the highest order that He would dare announce Himself as God's Messiah. And yet, even in His human normalcy, He was Who He announced Himself to be – Messiah, Savior, Deliverer! And whether or not He ever did any of His numerous signs and wonders, He was The miracle of God incarnate, tabernacled in normal human flesh.

He was, as the scripture says, the "firstborn among many brethren," and it is to this "many brethren" that we now focus our attention. Jesus said to Nicodemus that a man must be born again, born first of water and then born of the Spirit, in order to see and enter the kingdom of God. Nicodemus was incredulous at this, wondering what this could mean. His mind could not fathom it.

11

What Jesus meant, was that because of His incarnation and subsequent death and resurrection, the miracle of incarnation which was centered in Jesus, was to soon be reproduced and available to all of humanity for all time – the outpouring of the Spirit "upon all flesh" on the Day of Pentecost. All humanity from that point onward became potential recipients of the greatest miracle of all, the miracle of being born again of the Spirit of God.

Anyone who works in the Lord's vineyard knows what a miracle from heaven this is, far far surpassing all others. The reason is that it is much more an impossibility than other, flashier suspensions of the laws of the physical universe that we normally call miracles. A body is healed only to eventually perish. Sight is restored to physically blind eyes only to see those eyes one day shut in death. A man is raised from physical death only to die again later.

But this miracle of new birth has neither a beginning nor an end, because it does not come out of the space-time universe, is not subject to time and its laws, and produces something of far greater magnitude and infinitely more glory than anything else there is or ever could be. It is the long-ago sown seed of Christ, first implanted in Eve in the Garden, the Treader of the Serpent, first appearing "as the firstborn" in Jesus Christ of Nazareth, but NOW born again and growing up in normal human persons as we all are. "All heaven rejoices" at this, the scripture says, and it does not say that about anything else. Therefore, if this is the greatest joy of heaven, then surely it is the greatest miracle on earth.

This is it then, the greatest miracle of time and eternity: that fallen man, born in the law of sin and death from Adam, was raised up out of that death, even as was Jesus Who bore on Him the same death, to become the very sons of God. That He Who came as Son of Man and Son of God, would be reborn into every human who received Him, to be raised together with Him into the same heights and equality with God, and be co-heirs with Jesus of all that the Father has and is.

The second of these miracles, contained in the first, is the mystery of union, of Christ in us, the miracle of, "I live, yet it is not me, but Christ living."

12

Again, this is something we are unable to see with our physical eyes or hear with our physical ears, nor grasp with our reasoning human minds. It is utterly beyond the realm of human thinking or understanding. For most of us, this miracle is kept back in the beginning of our Christ-walk for a later fullness of time for us individually, when God again raises us up into Himself in understanding and consciousness. It is the seed of Christ grown up in us, so that as Christ has grown up in us ("Christ formed" in us as Paul said), even so we have grown up into Him.

It is coming to the understanding, fixed in our inner consciousness, of the complete doing away of the wall of separation between God and man, the total death of the "old man" we once were when we were under the domination of the serpent, and the rising up of the new creation in us in understanding and consciousness. We come to know that when people see us, they are seeing Jesus. We are enlightened to the fact that our humanity is holy, being the dwelling place of God in Three Persons, Father, Son and Holy Spirit, and that because when we walk we are He walking, now out of us begin to flow unstoppable rivers of Living Waters, for the healing of the nations.

When we were new born babes, we still did not know our oneness with God, and sought "things" from God as if He is apart and separate from us. But now, in this second of these miracles, we realize that we ourselves have become wells of Living Water, that the waters flow out of our middle, out of our center, because it is not we, but He! We become totally aware that as Jesus said, "Ye are the light of the world," we are, by virtue of the fact the He is the Light of the world, shining out of every fiber of our being, spirit, soul and body. We learn "as He is, so are we in this world," that the government (of our lives) is truly upon His shoulders, and we finally find rest from our own labors and now labor in the Lord outside our own strength and understanding, because He and we are one.

The third and final of these miracles, also contained in the first, is coming to a consciousness not only of Who we are, but also what we are about, and what our lives are for. It is to realize that as Christ is intercessor for all, we bear Him about in our bodies every moment of every day as intercessors with Him for the "perfecting of the saints," and "to present every man perfect in Christ Jesus."

This is because we have been taken into the holy of holies, into the innermost sanctuary, where we become so conscious of Who He is as a lamb slain in the midst of the Throne, that we cannot help ourselves but to be the same Lamb slain in the midst of the Throne within our own spirits. This is the fulfillment of "taking up His Cross and following Him." We now become Cross people, having no other purpose in life but to reproduce this eternal kingdom of other-love as God's appointed intercessors.

By intercessor I do not mean simply being a "prayer warrior" for others. That is only one aspect of intercession. But it is far more than that. After we have identified ourselves with Christ, bearing His identity now as our own, from that vantage point we begin to identify ourselves with other men and women, with their grieves and sorrows, as well as their joys and successes. They become our own, as if they are ours, now that we know we are He living and interceding by our broken humanity.

This is the final rung of the ladder that takes us out of self-focus. It is as if our Christian life has gone full circle at that point, and the incarnation of Jesus from Deity to Son of Man has fully taken us over. He knew He came to give His life as a ransom for many, and now we know the same. Because of Jesus' shed blood and broken body which effected our salvation and oneness with God, we know we cannot rest until we have attained to the resurrection of others! It is no longer our own resurrection we are concerned with, or even still less our level of piety or any other self-concern.

Jesus' constraint to accomplish the Father's plan in the Jerusalem now becomes our constraint. It takes us over and we can do no other. Finally we understand and enter into the greatest life of all, the life of Jesus in us being as a "corn of wheat falling into the ground to die .... which bringeth forth much fruit." For this purpose we are created and we can reach no further than being, as Paul the apostle said, "counted as sheep for the slaughter," and the fulfillment in us of Paul's glorious word of 1 Corinthians 4:9-13.

This is the life that Ole Henrik would introduce you to in the pages of this book. For me, Ole Henrik Skjelstad is a miracle of God. I have very rarely seen the life of Christ overtake someone so fast and so high as I have seen in Ole Henrik for only a little over a year. We met each other on Facebook of all places, he in Norway and me in Florida at the time. I saw that he was Paul Anderson-Walsh's friend, and that was good enough for me.

Immediately we began corresponding, a little slowly at first, but from across the Atlantic Ocean I could almost see the glory coming down on this humble, friendly and loving man. I could sense it. As the days and weeks went by, we corresponded more and more, and I could see the lights popping on in his being even though we were thousands of miles apart in space. In the Spirit we were with and in each other from the first.

A miracle is always a wonderful surprise. So meeting Ole Henrik was just such a surprise for me. I do not think I will ever get over it or that it will lose its sheen, as Moses transfigured face lost its glory.

Ole Henrik has discovered the endless glory, glory that does not face or diminish in any way, but instead brightens more and more as the days speed by.

This book is not like most other Christian books. It is not the regurgitation of learned dogma, but instead a living testimony of what "he has seen and heard" from God Himself. Ole Henrik is a miracle to me, and this book is a miracle for the world."

Fred Pruitt

"Ever since I was a teenager I have dreamed about publishing a book. I have written and published articles on my blogs for several years not thinking about them that they have the potential to be published in a different format. However, several of my readers have asked when I am to publish my first book. The seed was sown, and the idea that my articles could be compiled and published as a book has now become a reality. I had never imagined that my first book would be in English. However, God's ways are indeed different from ours. Every article is a result of my discovery of the pure grace message six years ago and not least that God during the summer of 2009 opened my eyes to the fact that I am in a union fellowship with Him. The book in many ways is a documentary of the discoveries I have been granted as I begun exploring the mystery – Christ in us. My hope and prayer is that this book may bless you in ways you hadn't thought possible. When Peter exclaimed: "You are the Christ, the Son of the living God", Jesus replied, "Flesh and blood has not revealed this to you, but my Father who is in Heaven." So it is with every new truth we are granted to behold in the infinite God – who is our Father and who has included us in His family."

Ole Henrik

Acknowledgements:

A huge thanks to my dear friend, Jessica Robertson, for her outstanding front cover illustration. I would also like to thank Fred Pruitt, author and preacher; DeeDee Winter, who is running normangrubb.com; Steve McVey, author, preacher, founder and leader of Grace Walk Ministries; and John Lynch, author, pastor, preacher and co-founder of True Faced, for their support and very kind words of introduction. I reckon all of them as very close and important friends. Check out their web pages:

www.thesingleeye.wordpress.com
www.normangrubb.com
www.gracewalk.org
www.truefaced.com

Crossing the River

And be not conformed to this world: but be ye transformed by the renewing of your mind, that ye may prove what is that good, and acceptable, and perfect, will of God. (Romans 12:2)

From the day we are born we are conditioned to think, sense and judge in accordance with appearances, that is, the natural world and how it presents itself. When we are born again it is vital that we learn how to perceive the kingdom of God which is contrary to everything we formerly know. Even if we have been involved in other religious systems which claim to know the spiritual world we need this renewal of the mind, because what characterize every religious system is self effort; what you must do to change, what you must do to satisfy the gods, how you must perform to make yourself acceptable to the deity.

The Old Testament conveys the most astounding and precious spiritual truths when the Spirit enlightens and renews our minds. Without this paradigm shift in our understanding this part of the Bible will remain nothing but pictures of lives lived and occurrences in ancient times. It will not render any deeper meaning than being a receipt for shoulds and oughts.

There came a day after forty years of wandering in the desert when the Israelites finally were in a position to cross the Jordan River (Joshua 1). But, Moses, representing the law, was not allowed to cross the river and had to die in the wilderness (Deut 32:48-52). The law's presence was banned from the Promised Land, which is Christ. So, when the people entered Canaan they entered Christ who has fulfilled the law in us.

The Promised Land was abounding with milk and honey and flourished with fruit the Israelites had not cultivated. This is a magnificent picture of the fruit of the Spirit which is manifested when we are in Christ. The fruit of the Spirit characterizes God and his being. Gal 5:22-23 is a description of God's perfect love, and which we through faith acknowledge is a mirror of us in our union with God. In the same manner as the Israelites received

17

the abundance of Canaan we receive the fruit of the Spirit when we are in Christ.

In the desert there was only bareness and hard work – there is no abundance of fruit when we are subject to the law. In the wilderness every man did what he thought was right in his own eyes (Deut 12:8), which denotes a Christian life of self effort and self reliance. In this religious system you are as holy as your best deeds. In Canaan holiness is imparted to you because of Christ (Hebr 10:14). We now clearly see that no fruit can grow and blossom under the law. In this system every self-effort will be devastated when tested by fire.

God led the Israelites to the threshold, but Joshua was the one who led the people across the river. They could dimly behold the realities of the new life ahead of them on the other side of the river, but they had to walk over themselves. The similarities to how we enter God's rest are stunning. This entering in is a conjunction of revelation and faith. We are given to see the shadows across the river (Deut 32:49), and we then take a leap of faith to possess what is our inheritance. Unbelief will cause us to continue our tedious march in the wilderness where the only thing which will sustain life is manna from above. But, when the diet has been manna for too long a period it grows bitter in the mouth , and this will be reflected in a person's whole being.

When you are in the desert you cannot return to Egypt and your unregenerate life, even though you long for those days when the law didn't condemn you. You long back to the evil taskmaster and the food he served you. But, the Red Sea is closed again. Your salvation is perpetually secured, but the desert doesn't offer much comfort or promise. You are saved, but you do not carry any fruit in the wilderness. In the Red Sea all the enemies who were against you, and who asserted ownership over you were obliterated. The Holy Spirit urges you to take the leap of faith into the unknown, but as the Israelites you are scared of what lies ahead. Those of us who have crossed the river can promise you one thing: Canaan really is overflowing with life and freedom in Christ.

Notice again that Moses had to die before anyone could enter the Promised Land. We cannot bring the law into Canaan, because there a different law operates; the law of life. It is only by the renewal of the mind that we can understand the spiritual realities which all are contrary to what we have always beheld in this natural, temporal world. We are unable to see grace and the union life – Christ in us – us in Christ, and our new identity in Him when we are in the desert. All these wonderful truths are obscured under the law, that is, in the wilderness.

Liberated Sons

There comes a day when we rediscover our "I" as a safe "I". We have been through the devastating stage when the law condemned us and ultimately caused us to come to the end of ourselves. Then we discovered to our great delight that we had died to the law. A new realization is now dawning upon us; we are in a union with the resurrected Christ. As we bask and revel in this wonderful truth another profound revelation is working its way through the surface and settles in our minds.

Our "I" reemerges as a safe "I". We discover that since we now are indwelled by God and are in Him everything pertaining to our being is cleansed, and we begin to experience the almost inexplicable liberty of being free sons who are perfectly expressing Him in our form. Every day we are carrying His death within, that is, our former conscious and subconscious thought patterns which have defined our personhood so long are fading and their defining power is shattered.

To enter this new life is a dying away from what we previously considered as our secure ground. To step out into the unknown is a terrifying and at the same time liberating experience, because now we finally are beginning to trust ourselves. Before we enter this level as fully operating persons we need to be completely settled in that God accepts and loves us.

Thus Jesus was assured by His father before He began His public service in earnest by these words: "This is my beloved Son, in whom I am well pleased." Jesus was now established as a safe Son who could say "I do nothing of myself" when He himself always was the doer. This paradox seems like a veil, until it is torn apart when we understand the depths of the union life. It is I, yet not I. It is He, and simultaneously it is me. We are one, and since I can trust Him I can trust myself.

I have found that I am a bit reluctant to step into the unknown and begin to operate as Him by, for instance, speaking out words of faith. God has to encourage me, and even push me over the cliff, either by using other persons or by speaking, Himself, to my heart. In Jesus' case God used Jesus' mother to push Him into operating as a safe liberated "I". At the wedding in Cana they ran out of wine and Jesus' mother challenged Him to do something about the situation. Jesus' harsh answer demonstrates His inner turmoil of entering a level formerly unknown to Him.

Then Jesus took a leap of faith and said His faith words: "Fill the waterpots with water". We know the rest of the story. But, notice what John writes after this incident: "…and manifested forth his glory". His glory, His "I" operating as a safe liberated son of the Most High trusting the promptings which surfaced in His thoughts and mind. Many of us are in this process of consciously becoming aware of that we are "co-saviours" with Christ as fully operating safe sons, that we are vessels of honor, that we are light and salt in this world. Not as a possibility, but as a fact!!!

His Joyful Pride

There is a cry in every human heart to hear the words: I am proud of you! Those words are in many ways the ultimate confirmation of our being. There are people who are so hungry to hear that they are an object of pride that they are willing to go to extremities. Neglect and deprivation have left many with a sense of worthlessness and meaninglessness.

We find as we behold the world that we are all unique. This craving for acceptance is something profounder than receiving ovations for what we do. We long to hear that someone will boast of and find pleasure in our unique existence, a recognition which supersedes our actions. However, it might seem to us that those who receive most attention in this world do so because of their accomplishments. Hence we make huge efforts to conform in an attempt to resemble our idols hoping some rain will fall upon us as well. As an effect we occur as false versions of our true personhood.

Due to the lie we compare and contrast our life with others and adapt to the prevalent culture, or we make an attempt to stand out by opposing it. There are days when the pain almost smoothers us and we find that activity and noise alleviate our ache. We are willing to go to great lengths to avoid rejection, and each moment we make another adaption our inner being becomes more entangled. To our surprise we discover that this cry in our heart doesn't diminish as we get older and supposedly more mature.

Every religious system that gives preference to works and appearances to mere being perpetuates the lie, and causes people to continue in bondage. Faith is the opposite of works. God has thus made faith prevalent in the new dispensation, because faith is an image of our innermost being where we are united in one spirit with the Godhead.

Our Father in heaven has through the image of his son experienced the same earthly afflictions as we encounter. He knows firsthand our emotions and soreness. Hence He is perfectly able to identify with his children in their quest for love. His desire to embrace and acknowledge His offspring is beyond words, and he displayed His eternal love and pride through the cross.

His sacrifice shouts out; I want you! It is a cry that qualifies our being as immensely significant to the creator of the universe. This goes far beyond our actions, because they are not impressive to Him who said: "I am." To be is the foundation for His pride in us. Therefore He perpetually meets every son with: "Well done, my child! Everything was against you, but despite your adversities you found your true being in my Son." His pride in us is displayed in a joy He cannot contain. He dances fervently and shouts out His joy every moment of our being. He pride in us causes Him to spin around under the influence of violent emotions (Zep 3:17).

Roots

A friend of mine once said something along these lines: The Holy Spirit has a huge job convincing people that they are perfect in Christ. I gave my approval, but I didn't quite understand how profound her statement was before now.

It seems like there exists a common misunderstanding among many believers which says that God has to fix the parts of my personality that I don't like. These personal traits make their presence known when we are facing some kind of affliction. We therefore assume that God leads us through these seasons in order to disclose the parts of us that need a fix.

When we are going through these periods we often experience some sort of condemnation which relates to our reactions and behavior. Wrongly we then think that The Holy Spirit is working in our lives to make us more like Jesus in terms of behavior.

The objective of these kinds of tribulations is, however, the opposite. God is showing us through them how deep the roots of condemnation go. When life is quiet and the world is smiling towards us it requires a simple act of faith to believe that we are perfect in Him. However, when the gale is coming our way our belief system is shaken.

When Jesus promised us liberty and an abundant life it is imperative that the roots of condemnation are exposed so that we can experience this quality of life. Condemnation cripples us, it robs us of our boldness and it makes life generally miserable. God cannot help us to accept the totality of His grace if we are not aware of these concealed roots which have found their way to the innermost places of our being. They can only be revealed when we are going through a tribulation which triggers patterns of reactions we despise and brings forth condemnation and shame. It is in this position of helplessness that the Holy Spirit can whisper His life-giving words to us.

We are in fact imitating Eve in the garden when we say that we are not perfect, and are in need of a fix. We really want to be good, and we often conclude that the new creation isn't perfect to the degree we had expected. We want God to better us so that we can resemble the image of Jesus we carry in our minds. If Eve hadn't found any faults with her being she wouldn't have been tempted to eat from the wrong tree.

When God says we are perfect He wants us to be secure in this truth. He encourages us to accept every part of us as a perfect image of Him without having any remnants of condemnation. This is a profound mystery, because when we accept ourselves as He accepts and loves us we find that our consciousnesses are expanded to embrace the fact that we are in Him as He is in us. He is the rivers of living water which effortlessly flow out of our hearts.

It is on this background that we can be happy when we face an affliction, because its sole purpose is to liberate us from shame which ruin our relationship with God, and it empowers us to clearly hear our Father say: "This is my beloved daughter/son in whom I am well pleased."

Faith

The "name and claim" theology was important in that sense that it brought forward faith as an important component of the Christian walk. The movement unearthed principles which are imperative in the new dispensation. I made a search for the word faith in NIV and got 286 hits, and that was just in the NT.

What caused the "name and claim" movement to flounder was that their understanding of faith was based on separation. The whole issue became a matter of own works and not resting in Christ. Separation in our context is me doing. Union, however, is Him doing in me as me. In this perspective we "name and claim" not to fulfill our own desires, but His desires, which is me for others, i.e. agape.

To believe that we now live in union is an issue of faith, that is, His faith imparted to us. However, His faith can be of no benefit if it's not received with faith. "For unto us was the gospel preached, as well as unto them: but the word preached did not profit them, not being mixed with faith in them that heard it." (Hebr 4:2)

In this position of faith His wants become our wants. His desires become our desires. When we believe this our faith has grown to a mature level and we are enabled to acknowledge Ephesians 4:5: "There is one Lord, one faith,…." " and Gal 2:20: "I am crucified with Christ: nevertheless I live; yet not I, but Christ liveth in me: and the life which I now live in the flesh I live by the faith of the Son of God, who loved me, and gave himself for me". Notice: "…by the faith of the Son….." Now we clearly see that His faith is our faith.

In other words we have the same faith as God. On what level does God's faith operate? Rom 4:17 provides the answer: ……before him whom he believed, even God, who quickeneth the dead, and calleth those things which be not as though they were.

Since Jesus was the firstborn of many sons and daughters we can with confidence state that He was an example of us. Jesus only did what He saw His Father do. How did He know what His Father was doing? He knew by faith. He had a profound understanding of and faith in that God perfectly expressed Himself through His son.

We also find Jesus exclaiming that He could do nothing of Himself, and further on, that He was in His father and His father in Him – evidently the union life. Trusting in faith in the indwelling life of the Father Jesus could do the most spectacular miracles without first having to go through a long period of ambivalence – is this just me, or is it you God?

Image

The consequences of the fall were many and its repercussions are still very vividly manifested in the human race. The inclination towards acting and being like God has many facets. One of the more subtle expressions is our desire to mold people in our image. We have expectations when it comes to how we want others to be or behave, how they live their lives and how they are to express their spiritual life through attitudes and works. When they fail to comply with our image we subtly or more directly begin to condition them applying a diversity of manipulation techniques from our copious arsenal.

Until our minds are renewed we have great difficulties in acknowledging and recognizing how God's master plan is unfolded uniquely in each individual. God employs the truth in His molding process. The truth which plainly and straight forward addresses the question; "who am I?". This truth is the definite truth, because the source is the Creator of all things. In telling us the unprecedented truth about our value and who we are in Him we are drawn close to this Person who is everything contrary to manipulative. In this truth we breathe freely and in an instant we become this truth through faith.

The paths He leads us to follow are everything the religious world is not. When we fell our preconceived opinions concerning how things ought to be were formed according to the ideas of the ruler we now had submitted to. The record is very brief when it comes to what life in the garden was like. We only catch some glimpses of Eve and Adam having an intimate relationship with their Father. There is a great secret contained in this, because in this silence the potential of true liberty is. God doesn't have to abide to a receipt in His dealings with His precious children.

So, when you ask God, as Peter did, why He leads someone in a direction you don't approve of He will answer: "……. what is that to thee? follow thou me" (John 21:22). Jesus' answer might seem harsh, but if we are to paraphrase it would be something like this: "Peter, everything I do is love and my love manifests itself uniquely in each and every individual.

Therefore everyone will be led along different paths where they can trust me completely, because everything is woven in love." However, there is also an edge to His words, because if we are trapped in a rigid pattern of comparing ourselves with others we will not easily yield to His perfect ways.

To compare ourselves with others denotes that we still haven't entered His rest and His freedom. It falls thus natural for us to deny others to enter this liberty when we haven't tasted it ourselves, and the temptation to begin molding others in our image is irresistible. In doing so we are proclaiming that we do not respect the individual, we do not understand love and we are unwilling to let others flourish in His light.

Rest

"In that day shall this song be sung in the land of Judah; We have a strong city; salvation will God appoint for walls and bulwarks. Open ye the gates, that the righteous nation which keepeth faith may enter in" (Isaiah 26:1-2)

Isaiah must have been a tad surprised over this, because what he passed on says that those who keep faith will enter the new city of salvation. He might have been a bit dumbfounded as well hearing God utter something contrary to what he had been reared to obey, because the covenant he was subjected to demanded perfection under the law to enter God's salvation.

We all know that failing to observe the commandments and the law was called sin under the old covenant. Sin in the new dispensation must thus be not keeping faith. Paul confirms this in Rom 14:23: "For whatsoever is not of faith is sin."

My conclusion is obviously that we are not to be concerned with our works, doings, attitudes and so forth, but be preoccupied with faith only – which is Christ, who He is and who we are in Him. The reason why Jesus left us with His peace is found in verse 12 in Isaiah 26: "LORD, thou wilt ordain peace for us: for thou also hast wrought all our works in us." Let us all enter His rest through faith, because it is finished!

Rest II

We have established that under the new covenant sinning was to not keep faith (Isa 28:2). David also foresaw that it would come a time when sins no longer would be the issue in man's relation to God: "Blessed are they whose iniquities are forgiven, and whose sins are covered. Blessed is the man to whom the Lord will not impute sin." (Rom 4:7-8)

It is quite clear that David's words relate to the believer, because John said: "Whoever has been born of God does not sin, for His seed remains in him; and he cannot sin, because he has been born of God." (1 John 3:9) In this context we can understand the following words penned down by Paul on a more profound level: There is therefore now no condemnation to them which are in Christ Jesus, who walk not after the flesh, but after the Spirit. (Rom 8:1)

It is now obvious that a person who cannot sin cannot experience any condemnation either, particularly now that we are aware of that sin is related to faith and nothing else. The believer lives by faith, because he has accepted Christ and is born again. Nothing he will ever do will be counted against him. This is pure and undefiled grace! It is unfathomable for the unregenerate spirit, and also for many of those who are still in their childhood, spiritually speaking.

Paul said: "And all things are of God, who hath reconciled us to himself by Jesus Christ, and hath given to us the ministry of reconciliation; To wit, that God was in Christ, reconciling the world unto himself, not imputing their trespasses unto them; and hath committed unto us the word of reconciliation. Now then we are ambassadors for Christ, as though God did beseech you by us: we pray you in Christ's stead, be ye reconciled to God.

27

For he hath made him to be sin for us, who knew no sin; that we might be made the righteousness of God in him. " (2 Cor 5:18-21)

The unbeliever is thus still in sin because he hasn't yet accepted Christ in faith. However, he is just a simple step from being declared righteous and be reconciled to God, just as we are.

As we all know Jesus never sinned. When John states: "Herein is our love made perfect, that we may have boldness in the day of judgment: because as he is, so are we in this world." (1 John 4:17) it is also an argument for our perfection. If we are in this world as He is, and He was and is found without sin, then we also are found without sin in this temporary world. When this verse speaks about love it is quite obvious that John refers to God's love which now is perfected through His unprecedented grace.

The Tower of Babel

One of the greatest, most scandalous and dangerous lies which is preached in the church is that we must become more like Jesus. That was the lie which ruined Eve and Adam's relationship with God. All because Eve believed the lie that she needed to become more like God. Notice that after the fall it wasn't God who withdrew from those two. It was Eve and Adam who hid themselves from God. Shame had entered paradise. This rather persistent feeling renders us with a feeling of nakedness, of not belonging and it alienates us from recognizing our Heavenly Father's love.

Shame is the means by which the prince of the power of the air controls and conditions his doomed kingdom. It is this feeling of disgrace that shame promotes which inhibits every man from being a true image of the Godhead. Shame cripples, ruins and it causes man to hide from God. Jesus never exhorted anyone to be like Him, because that would be to contradict and thwart His royal mission.

He came to expose the lie, atone for its consequences and provide liberty for the captives. The fall had rendered man spiritually blind. Man firmly believed that He had to improve himself so he began comparing himself with the creation. He found that he was superior to everything else in it, except his fellow man. The next step was thus to compare and contrast himself with his peers so that he could be the foremost among them.

Man began erecting his own righteousness, the tower of Babel. It was a bold and ambitious project which only outcome would be to entrench man in his delusion and reinforce the hold of the lie. So, God did what He does in every person's life. He destroyed the tower and scattered man's righteousness to the extent that it was completely leveled. This is the story of every man.

Shame's twin brother condemnation has caused too many believers to bow their head with a urgent sense of falling short, simply because someone has passed on an idea of a standard which resembles the tower of Babel, that is, the original lie presented in different words. We are rendered feeling useless, of no value and a hindrance to God, because of our imagined shortcomings. We don't feel loving, we don't feel spiritual, and compared to others we seemingly do not have the brilliant gifts which they are endowed with.

Accepting ourselves is vital if we are to recognize ourselves as perfect images of Christ in our form. It was God who chose us. It was solely His initiative to gather us as a family of many sons. He chose us exactly as we are with every human facet we have. If He has accepted us we can accept ourselves. Not doing so is in fact an insult against His sober judgment.

Chasing our own righteousness is the basic sin which prevents us from becoming what we were created to be; ourselves. As a substitute we become a distorted version of ourselves. When we aren't ourselves we are nothing. There is only one truth and only one righteousness which restore our true being; His.

Before the fall Eve and Adam perfectly expressed themselves. The day they ate of the fruit they became expressions of sin, and God plainly told them that their lives from now on would be a perpetual struggle to be something they never could be in their own powers. Originally they were furnished with faith faculties to be faith people. A life outside God was destined to be a life of appearances.

Only spirit people can discern spiritually and make righteous judgments. Thus the new creation is a partaker of divine nature. Such a person doesn't judge in accordance with outward realities. He sees behind outer success, prestige, influence and affluence. That person clearly sees the emptiness in the hearts of those who are wise in this world. As a result a faith person does not pursue those things. He isn't easily deceived by worldly things. What motivates him is the love of God which is outpoured into His heart. His passion is Christ, and nothing this world has to offer holds any appeal to him.

Faith involves the competence of seeing beyond appearances and accepting God's truth about us as the final truth. If He says we are love, because He is love, that is a fact despite our circumstances or what we imagine we behold with our earthly eyes. The day we acknowledge that we in Christ are everything we are meant to be in this temporal realm we are set completely free to express ourselves without shame or any other crippling emotion.

David and Saul

An interesting episode in the scripture with great significance for us is that David was elected king while Saul still was the anointed king of Israel. During a period of several years they were both kings over the Promised Land. Saul was big, handsome and strong. He exuded all the qualities a genuine king was supposed to have.

Saul's reign was apparent to all of his people. David, however, was more or less unknown and invisible to most. He only gathered a handful of men who were loyal to him and who recognized him as the true king over the nation. When we now are to investigate which significance this has for our lives we will consider Saul as a type of our fleshy inclinations whilst David represents the union life.

From the moment we are born again we are kings and royal priest in the kingdom of God. In the beginning of our walk we are like Saul. We are the perfect image of self effort and fleshy patterns which we hope will make us presentable to God. Our good deeds are handsome in our eyes. We cherish our strengths and we ask God to bless our works.

Simultaneously there is a David within waiting for Saul to die, so that the one who is a man after God's heart can step forward to occupy the throne. The man who lives after the flesh will finally come to the end of himself. His efforts have been utterly rejected by God. All he has left is his faith, and the faith person who has been there all the time, but has been more or less invisible because he has been repressed by the flesh, steps forth.

Saul, the religious archetype, trusted his own strength. David, on the other hand, put his trust in God alone. But even in our "Saul" period David is given the opportunity from time to time to take precedence, notably when Saul is facing a challenge to big for him. So David pokes his head forth and through faith kills the Goliaths which threatens to overthrow Saul. However, Saul isn't convinced that this weakling which he to a certain degree despises will secure his reign. He thus continues his life ignoring the power of the faith seed which is disseminated and which at last will conquer and overshadow the flesh.

Norman Grubb denotes this revelation when we discover that we are in a union with Christ the second crisis. We go from this false idea of separation, that is, God here and me there to a secure position of knowing that we know that we are joined one spirit with Him. This insight or revelation turns everything we formerly believed more or less upside down. The scriptures are opened to us in new ways. We begin to see and understand things which have been hidden from us because of our Saul life.

The good news is that there exist a David in every believer who is groaning in anticipation to be liberated and step up as a secure and safe son of His father. He has been a secure and beloved son from the beginning, but He hasn't recognized it before now. Glorious and joyful is every son who knows who he is in Christ.

To be in the flesh denotes the erroneous idea that we live apart from Christ. This understanding leads to self-effort and a thinking which is sin conscious in its outlook. It is also apt to downgrade our soul and our soul reactions. We can also attribute to the flesh the idea that some soul reactions are more noble than others, which means a division in good and evil. Our soul is "fearfully and wonderfully made." In Christ it again has found its perfection, its original design.

Fleshy thinking patterns will obstruct the believer from accepting himself as God has accepted him and impede the believer's ability to recognize who he is in Christ. We now clearly recognize that the flesh represents a false idea of separation. This unsound idea of independence leads to "shoulds" and "ought tos". The flesh thus perpetuates condemnation and suffocates faith.

Saul, "who was little in his own eyes", is a typical representative of those fleshy thinking patterns which results in a desire to prove oneself, whilst David, "a man after God's heart, represents faith and its restful position in Christ.

Into His Likeness

For whom he did foreknow, he also did predestinate to be conformed to the image of his Son, that he might be the firstborn among many brethren. (Rom 8:29)

What does it mean to be conformed into the likeness of Jesus Christ? We can immediately dismiss any notion that it has something to with physical likeness.

Before we continue our investigation let us notice that those God foreknew are predestined to be conformed to His likeness. This is a promise, something which inadvertently will come through because it is a work of the Spirit. We make it much easier for ourselves if we immediately yield to His mighty work in us, and not harden our hearts like the Israelites in the wilderness. We are of course in this context talking about faith and not self-effort.

Faith encourages, no more than that, it compels us to live from a position of rest which denotes a being characterized by spontaneity. This is the Spirit perfectly leading us in our daily lives to be ourselves, our true image of Him where we do right because it is His life which is manifested through mortal flesh.

In my dealings with people I have never met anyone who has identical behavior, thought patterns or reactions. People have equally different gifts. They have different personalities and they can differ quite a lot on particular issues. I assume that is the intention with Christ's body where every member has different functions. Despite our differences Jesus specifically prayed that we all should be one as He and His Father are one. I thus infer that being conformed to the likeness of Him has nothing to do with that we all are to act identical.

We can of course be tempted to judge this matter in behavior terms only. In order words to be transformed into His likeness means unisonely that all Christians are to be recognized by their good deeds and good works. There is a morsel of truth in this assumption, I believe. However, I do not think this either is the answer to our question plainly because Jesus quite firmly dismissed the idea that He was good. "Only One is good", He answered his opponents. When the devil attempted to tempt Him to do something to prove that He was God's son He adamantly refused to be defined by what He did. His identity was based on being.

Jesus ministry was categorized by many and stunning miracles. So far I have not come across anyone with this capacity to work miracles. There have been and are persons, though, who have had and have an extraordinary anointing on this field, but none of those can claim that everyone who came to them were healed from their ailments. So, this is it not either.

Jesus' redemptive work was the trademark of His ministry. It thus makes sense to me that when we are searching for an answer to our question this might be an important key when it comes to recognizing what it means to be conformed to His likeness in this temporal realm. There is only one Savior, only one who deliberately died on a cross to save the world. However, if we are to carry our crosses it must mean that we somehow are co-saviours operating in the Spirit to those who are granted us. This of course includes to a certain degree, as most of us have experienced, both tribulations and suffering.

Who would have known that a man hanging on a cross would alter the whole course of the Universe? That a rather insignificant incident in a tucked away place would have such immense consequences? It is almost ludicrous to consider. Well, if God could use such an odd method to save the world, it wouldn't be surprising if He would use rather insignificant and unusual means to make us co-saviours of our universe, would it? He is God, He can use anything to His glory. Perhaps we have some rather unrealistic and erroneous ideas on how we are to impact our surroundings?

Jesus was the firstborn of many sons. Sons denote plurality and diversity. I attended a concert the other day, where the main attraction in one of his songs sang a duet with a female vocalist. Their voices were in perfect harmony and they perfectly complemented each other. However, the audience didn't have any problems distinguishing the two voices. Together they spellbound the audience. Separately those two had great voices, but put together they reached levels of beauty they couldn't have attained on their own. If he had sung duets with others the effect would have been the same, but with a different ring. In addition his voice was so strong that he would have lifted anybody to new levels of harmony and euphony. The universe is reverberating with duets of different rings where one of the singers always is the same.

He is eternal life, love, power and all the other wonderful things we associate with Him. When John in his first epistle asserts that as He is so are we in this world that plainly denotes that we also are those things which He is. This absolutely implies being conformed into His likeness. John also tells us that "in the beginning was the word, and the word was with God." The word "with" denotes in Greek a position which best can be described as being "face to face." Into His likeness thus means that we are face to face with God. We are hence talking about the restoration of the intimacy of the Garden.

Kokichi Kurosaki puts it like this: "God created man in His likeness, a spiritual being capable of responding to His love and having koinonia with Him."

True Assessment

Wherefore henceforth know we no man after the flesh: yea, though we have known Christ after the flesh, yet now henceforth know we him no more. Therefore if any man be in Christ, he is a new creature: old things are passed away; behold, all things are become new. And all things are of God, who hath reconciled us to himself by Jesus Christ, and hath given to us the ministry of reconciliation. (2 Cor 5:16-18)

Despite the fact that we are declared as new creations in the scriptures we rarely feel that way. It seems to us that we still are the same old person doing the same old things thinking the same thoughts we always have.

This is all a question of appearances, isn't it? The new creation is new through and through. It can't be regarded or judged according to the flesh. It belongs to a different realm. It is a spiritual being manifested in soul and body. What a wonderful gift it is when we are imparted to see beyond appearances and behold our true self in faith. The self which is one spirit with its Father. The self He has beheld from before the foundation of the universe.

What a beautiful picture of ourselves we see when our consciousnesses are renewed to the true image of our being. The image He holds up as a mirror. This is the image we are transformed into beholding with our spiritual eyes as we go from glory to glory. We see beyond appearances in our own life and we begin to see the beauty in others as well, because finally we have arrived to the place where we accept and love ourselves with the same acceptance and love our Father has toward us in all His dealings with us.

In a process of the renewal of our minds we have put off everything which pertains to that old self, which really wasn't a self. It was just a distorted version composed of lies. In this process we rediscover ourselves and find to our surprise that we are just as He is. In the same manner as we have found peace with Him we have found peace with ourselves.

This desire to change, to better ourselves has dissolved into nothing, because it was nothing. We are everything God says we are. We have given up that old self and its distorted view of its being and found our new life. In the realm of appearances it might look the same, but it isn't. We perhaps continue to do the things we always have done. We work, we watch TV, we eat and we sleep. This is life! This is the perfect version of ourselves.

He was just a simple carpenter from Nazareth, but He was God's son! What everything boils down to is this; who is your father? What spirit are you of? He has cleansed us once and for all, and thus, for the pure everything is pure. It is all of grace! What an incredible mystery this is; He united to us living as us in a world seemingly full of paradoxes to the unskilled eye. We are one, yet two.

But as it is written, Eye hath not seen, nor ear heard, neither have entered into the heart of man, the things which God hath prepared for them that love him. (1 Cor 2:9)

Transformations/Repentance

To repent = μετανοέω = think differently or afterwards, that is, reconsider. The Greek word also carries the meaning of aligning ones thoughts with God's.

My different repentance experiences have been as follows:

From New Age to Jesus. That was a relief because I didn't have to save myself any longer.
From law to grace. That was indeed a tremendous relief.
From the idea that God was stingy, to seeing His generosity. Boy, that was a relief.
When I grasped that even sanctification wasn't a work of mine, I was immensely relieved.
When I understood that God isn't angry I became very, very relieved.
When I discovered the mystery, Christ in me; I was relieved beyond measure.
When I have had glimpses of my inheritance as a son, I have been joyfully relieved.
Each new discovery about the height and the width of God's love has been reassuringly relieving.
Finding out I was dead was a dreadful relief, but being raised up as a new creation was a supernatural relief.
Discovering my new identity was a wonderful relief.
When I was convinced that my salvation was eternally secured, I became relaxingly relieved.

My experience has been that repentance equals experiencing relief. Instances when I have repented in the religious sense of the word (i.e. remorse, regret, and etc.) have almost, without exception, been a disaster because it has led to rededication; new promises and more works to satisfy a Person who already is gratified. In retrospect, I can see that those instances did not change me a tad.

He has transformed me, and each transformation has been a consequence of love followed by a sigh of relief on my part.

Blind, but Now Seeing

"And he cometh to Bethsaida; and they bring a blind man unto him, and besought him to touch him. And he took the blind man by the hand, and led him out of the town; and when he had spit on his eyes, and put his hands upon him, he asked him if he saw ought. And he looked up, and said, I see men as trees, walking. After that he put his hands again upon his eyes, and made him look up: and he was restored, and saw every man clearly." *(Mark 8:22-25)*

When you have a desire to see dear ones saved you pray to your heavenly Father and He will send Jesus to them. Jesus will take the hand of the blind person and lead him to a place where He can manifest Himself and endow the gift of regeneration unto him.

In the beginning the new creation will behold the newness of his being with childish eyes. He will have an understanding that his sins are forgiven, and that something has happened within. His spiritual sight will, however, be blurred, and this will be manifested through his aptness to follow the habits of the old man attempting to make himself presentable to God by his own works.

But it is Jesus who does everything, and who will ask the new man when his resources are exhausted; "Do you see anything?", that is, do you appreciate that you are a new creation whose old man died on the cross with me? When I say died, I mean both those parts of you that you found repulsive and those parts in which you were proud. Do you know that both your "evil" and your "good" are nothing? Do you know that I am here to live in you through you as you? Do you know that I am the only One who can live the Christian life? Do you know that you also are resurrected with me to take part in my resurrection life?

It is now that Jesus put the final touch on His work in that person's life. He opens his eyes so that he can behold clearly the beauty of the union life with Christ and enjoy his life as a perfect manifestation of the invisible God.

We have all gone from spiritual blindness to an intermediate position where things are a bit blurred, and from here we are firmly steered to the final revelation where we with increasingly clarity behold the magnificence of God's plan. We are perfectly saved also in our state of childishness when we strive in our ignorance, but as our consciousnesses are renewed to the image of Christ we are transformed from glory to glory.

Notice that it is Jesus who is the doer. The man merely follows along, puts his trust in Jesus and answers a simple question. Obviously, the blind man could have refused Jesus' offer to lead him out of the village, that is, his old self and old life. He could have lied to Jesus and retorted that his present sight was adequate, or perfectly suitable for his kind of life; that he was satisfied with his condition.

The spit symbolizes Jesus' life now imparted to the man. In John 9:6 we find that Jesus spat on the ground and made mud that he smeared on the eyes of a man who was born blind, which is a common human condition, spiritually speaking. God formed man from dust of the ground (Gen 2:7), so when Jesus mixes His salvia with the dust this is a powerful image of the union life.

The Journey

There is no fear in love; but perfect love casteth out fear: because fear hath torment. He that feareth is not made perfect in love. (1 John 4:18)

There was a time in my life when the fear of death cast dark shadows over my existence. The sting of death was an almost daily nuisance and it rendered my soul to shrink in fear whenever it found an opportunity to bite. This sensation of helplessness aroused a spiritual hunger which at first led this stranger to the spiritual realm to explore Eastern philosophies for an answer. Karma and reincarnation seemed as plausible explanations to the big questions which death aroused. Even though the puzzle seemingly had found its consummation, fear reigned in the mind of the newly converted New Age adherent.

It wasn't that the new philosophies encouraged towards much self-effort and an idea of bettering oneself that perpetuated this crippling feeling. I was ready to do anything necessary to qualify for a better existence in my next life. Fear plainly was a faithful companion during those years, and it caused soul pain and palpitations. I thought those manifestations would be history as soon as I had entered a more profound understanding of the spiritual realities I explored. Fear most likely was caused by imbalances in my yin and yangs. It would thus be a splendid idea to balance the Chakras. Unfortunately I didn't have the crystals which would accelerate the process.

It is now God finds it opportune to interfere and begin convincing me about His existence, and He adds that there merely is one way to eternal life, and that is His son Jesus Christ. Since He is very persistent and persuasive I discovered that everything I believed in was wool. It could to a certain degree keep me warm, but it was without any substance. Fear now lost some of its grip. It wasn't longer bothering me in a palpable physical way. However, I was afraid that if I didn't do the right things and pleased my new master He would abandon me in disgust and anger. Hence, this rather ambitious and strong-willed son did His very best to live the new life in accordance to the guidelines He found in the scriptures and what other told him was necessary.

When I came to the end of myself I did so with a bang that most likely reverberated through the universe for several minutes. To walk in a depressive darkness is very instructive. It kind of prepares you for God's grace. So when the revelation came that I was dead to the law and that His blessings were chasing me new hope and life were infused into this poor soul. There was a new lightness to my steps. The sun was shining again and life seemed promising. However, God was still up there and I was stuck here. I still wasn't persuaded that my salvation was eternally secured, so there were still moments when fear found a crack in the defense and bit. I still wasn't perfected in love.

God, however, had another surprise up His sleeve. He plainly told me that when I was born again I entered a union with Him; an indissoluble unity which would last forever. Christ thus lived my life as me and I was a perfect expression of Him. In other words, the mystery revealed. We might be tempted to think that Ole Henrik now was completely free and fearless. Dear reader, please do not hasten to immature conclusions, because Ole Henrik is a complicated guy. A new issue materialized: Can I completely trust my soul reactions even though I am in this union? Am I love as He is love? It was time for the Spirit to teach me about how appearances and erroneous mindsets regarding Jesus still kept me in bondage.

To see love perfected in a person denotes that a person's faith reaches beyond the fact that God is love, that He is all in all and that everything works out for good for those who love Him and begins to trust himself. God is my keeper. He ingeniously utilizes my soul reactions to reach others through me. I am not always conscious of how His is doing that. I am merely myself with everything that entails. I do not longer judge my emotions or doings as good or evil. I have discovered that I am. I know that my Father cherishes challenges, and I somehow know that I have been an enjoyable challenge to Him. I can vividly imagine how He is smiling His best smile to me as I am settled in this magnificent truth. He probably says something along these lines: "Well, Ole Henrik, so here we are. It has been quite a journey, but now you have finally found your life again. We are companions, you know! I am in you and you in Me. But, the best is yet to come."

Discernment

And be not conformed to this world: but be ye transformed by the renewing of your mind, that ye may prove what is that good, and acceptable, and perfect, will of God. (Rom 12:2).

In our formative days, before we got to know Christ, and later when we observed the law, we had a clear idea of what was good and what was evil. This knowledge was derived from the tree of good and evil. We thought we were like God and judged accordingly. In the new dispensation we get, however, an increasingly understanding that eating from the forbidden tree equals spiritual death, and we will ultimately turn to the tree of life, which is Christ.

Those notions which we learned in our childhood days still influence our ability to discern. We are often enticed to assess from this obsolete perspective. It is when we encounter grace that everything changes. Moral and ethics which are powered from the tree of good and evil we come to understand are void conceptions in the liberty of the spirit. We need new perspectives of judging ourselves, the temporal world and the spiritual world.

God made man in His image. Man reflected God from the outset perfectly. God gave man some faculties which would manifest God, the spirit, in a material world. Man was given emotions. He could express joy, happiness, tranquility, love, desire, anger, hate, irritation and so forth. When Adam fell man began to consider some of his faculties more prominent than others. We began to discern between good feelings and bad feelings. Some of our emotions were considered more noble than others. We classified what we did; either as good or evil.

In the new dispensation, however, we can no longer judge our emotions or what we do according to our preconceived notions. By faith we now come to accept every part of us as a perfect expression of God. Because everything is now determined by which spirit who dwells in us and reigns in our lives. More than that; if we live in separation, that is, me for God, this will be our vantage point, and our aptitude to discern will be immature.

By the renewal of our mind we will as the spirit leads come to acknowledge by faith that we live in union with God. He in us and we in Him. It is here that we are enabled to discern what the will of God is, and He is more than capable of expressing Himself through every single faculty we are furnished with. As a consequence we completely accept our soul and its diversity.

It is no longer a question about which emotion is most noble, but which emotion God expresses Himself through in this particular situation. We come to hate what God hates, we find joy in the same things that delight God. We cry with those who grieve. We speak harshly to those we are led to oppose. This spirit led life is impossible to comprehend when we are eating from the tree of good and evil. Paul put it like this; "Which things also we speak, not in the words which man's wisdom teacheth, but which the Holy Ghost teacheth; comparing spiritual things with spiritual." (1 Cor 2:13).

We are now beginning to eat solid food as the author of the epistle to the Hebrews observed ; "But strong meat belongeth to them that are of full age, even those who by reason of use have their senses exercised to discern both good and evil." (Hebr 5:14). We need constant practice, because it takes time come to terms with a new reality, and God is our teacher in this process.

If we judge life by our old measuring stick we are an easy prey to erroneous believes. Basically we can say that evil in this new context of life is everything which are not of God. What we earlier judged as good, is not necessarily good in an eternal perspective. It is only in Him that we are enabled to understand that everything we encounter in this life is an opportunity for Him to be glorified through us.

Everything done from separation, that is, my works, no matter how noble, perpetuates the illusion of not being in a living spontaneous union with our

Father. Every beacon we navigated after are, thus, now gone. To our dilemma there is only one solution; accepting by faith that we are in union with God, that we are perfected in Him and that as He is in this world so are we. Here we can rest and let Him perfect His work in us and express Himself through us.

Where His Glory Dwells

But this shall be the covenant that I will make with the house of Israel; After those days, saith the LORD, I will put my law in their inward parts, and write it in their hearts; and will be their God, and they shall be my people. (Jer 31:33)

I remember those days very vividly when I still thought that the law was something which I had to observe by self effort. The law was something outside me which I as a good Christian had to fulfill. What an anguish my soul went through when I repeatedly failed. I still carried around this illusion that God and I were separate beings; He there and I here. I firmly believed that He would give me power to overcome my apparent shortcomings. I must admit I was a bit confused when that power never materialized.

I have, however, come to realize that Christ lives inside me as me, which of course is a huge mystery; that we who are two are one spirit joined together. He will not give me power to overcome anything, since He is power. It isn't something He has so that He can dispense it to needy Christians. He is power, and it is only through realizing our union that I become power as He is power. It was only by me failing miserably that He could reveal to me that this is the new reality. That illusion of separation really had my mind in a tight grip, so I had to come to the end of myself before I ceased making so much noise.

Lately I have been fascinated by Paul's statement in Romans 8:4; "That the righteousness of the law might be fulfilled in us, who walk not after the flesh, but after the Spirit." A verse which corresponds wonderfully with Jeremiah 31:33. In the new covenant the law isn't longer something out there which I have to adhere to. It is something which is fulfilled in me, because it is God who works in me, both to will and to work for his good pleasure.

Notice that Paul says "might be fulfilled in us" in the verse quoted from the Romans. Now it becomes very interesting, because that little preposition "in" denotes in Greek to be in from a position of rest! Hence, all my struggling to perform impeded His ability to fulfill the law in me and through me as me! There was no room for Him to spontaneously express Himself through my mortal flesh when my life was governed by rigid rules.

Paul had quite a struggle with the Galatians. After they had come to Christ some wolves had infiltrated their church and promoted the law as a necessary ingredient in the new life. Frustrated Paul exclaimed: "My little children, of whom I travail in birth again until Christ be formed in you." (Gal 4:19). Here Paul is saying the same thing as He did to the Romans, but in different words due to a different context. Trying to live the Christian life impedes Christ being formed in us!

To a rather huge group of well meaning Christians that must come as a big shock. We have heard more often than what we wish to count that we have to become more like Christ. That was the original sin from Eden; trying to become more like God. The law is a perfect and holy expression of God's character. Attempting to live in accordance to the law is thus repeating the original lie. Hence Paul writes to the Galatians: "For all who rely on works of the law are under a curse."

What does it mean that Christ is formed in us? I have come to understand that this is finding our lives again in Him to be perfect expressions of Him in our uniqueness. I am liberated to fully be myself with everything that entails. That is both a profound and magnificent gift. In this lies the realization that I am fearfully and wonderfully made to be an expression of the divine life as me. Only the Spirit can settle us in this truth through faith.

Our old master, Satan, is expelled from the temple. Thus I now say as the psalmist: "LORD, I have loved the habitation of thy house, and the place where thine honour dwelleth." (26:8). That place is me.

Stand up and Walk

I don't think Peter knew how profound his words were when he healed the crippled beggar by exclaiming: "Silver and gold have I none; but such as I have give I thee: In the name of Jesus Christ of Nazareth rise up and walk." Recently filled by the Spirit he and the other disciples with boldness expressed the new power which had found a dwelling place in their cleansed temples.

At that time Peter couldn't have apprehended the full scope of the words he uttered. It wasn't until later that he received the revelation that the gospel was for the Gentiles as well. It was Paul who was elected to receive the full revelation of the union life, which would propel Paul to take the leap of faith where he completely indentified himself with our Father and perceived that he was an expression of Christ in his form. This is what Norman Grubb calls the total truth of our being, recognizing the Other as the source of our workings and doings.

It was most likely Paul who passed on his revelation to Peter. We find that Peter in one of his letters alludes to this when he mentions that some of the things Paul writes in his letters are difficult for many to comprehend. Despite Peter's ignorance about the union life in the beginning of his ministry the Spirit spoke those faith words of healing through him for a special purpose. Unfortunately, many have interpreted his utterance as a magic formula on how to minister healing to people. However, that was not the Spirit's intention.

Those words plainly symbolize that when we recognize Christ within we understand that we operate in His resurrection power as His representatives on this planet. This identification from the Spirit's standpoint is so inclusive that He beholds us as perfect expressions of the divine life, and thus ambassadors for Christ who boldly can speak words of faith with the authority of the Father spontaneously when it swells up in us. As Paul and Peter we also can enter this fixed inner spirit reality of who we really are when that illusion of self improvement is shattered. However, as was the case for Peter we don't need to have a full understanding of this to be used mightily by God to further His kingdom.

Let us now take this a step further. We know by experience and many witnesses that God still heals, and that is wonderful. There is, however, an issue that is far more important than physical healing. There are plenty of Christians who still are crippled by condemnation and self introspection. They are rendered lame and cannot walk in the freedom Christ purchased for everyone of us who believe in His name. We are thus commissioned, as Peter so vividly demonstrated, to talk our word of faith to those who are crippled by law and self effort to walk in Him!

That is the real healing that will last throughout eternity!

Our True Origin

Jesus boldly proclaimed: "He that hath seen me hath seen the Father." (John 14:19). To the disciples he explains that this is true because He is in the Father and the Father is in Him. Jesus also says that to acknowledge this is a matter of faith. The religious mob, that is, those who live by appearances and not faith, found it both appalling and blasphemous when Jesus likened Himself with God.

When John in 1 John 4:8 says that God is love we are inclined to believe him despite the seeming darkness which surrounds us. A question which is reasonable to ask in this context is; what is love? Since Jesus was the image of God and God is love it becomes quite clear that the most powerful display of love ever was the crucifixion.

Love in its purest form is love for others. The cross is God's heart displayed for all to see. His love for others in such a driving force in everything He undertakes that it casts out every fear in the recipients and establish a secure ground on which we can relate to our heavenly Father. When His love is for us – we have established this is love that sacrifices itself for others – what can then separate us from Him? His love will perpetually seek our best, but most of all it will seek our hearts, because this is His heart's passion manifested in Christ. His desire to join His heart with His precious children is like an irresistible flood. Nothing can prevent it from attaining its eternal purposes.

Why could Jesus exclaim that those who had seen Him had seen the Father? The child who was conceived by Mary was from the Holy Spirit. Jesus was born of God. He was the firstborn and foremost of many sons. Every Christian is born again by the Spirit, and thus a son. The Father is not ashamed of his sons. They are new creatures, and He clearly see who we really are, namely spirit persons, and that is also our original true origin.

In Him the invisible God is made visible again; in order that every one may recognise their true origin in Him, He is the firstborn of every creature. (In Him we clearly see the mirror reflection of our original image and likeness.) (Col 1:15 – Mirror Translation)

Christ is formed in us when we renounce self-effort and self-reliance, that is, the law (Gal 4:19) and embrace His grace, which is Christ. His love is manifested in us with increasingly intensity as we are transformed from glory to glory until we one day find that we also are willing to sacrifice life itself for the benefit of others knowing beyond any doubts that there is a new body and an eternity in His presence awaiting.

By faith we can say: "Whoever has seen me has seen Christ." Simply because we are in Him and He is in us.

Rest through Faith

For if Jesus had given them rest, then would he not afterward have spoken of another day. There remaineth therefore a rest to the people of God. For he that is entered into his rest, he also hath ceased from his own works, as God did from his. Let us labour therefore to enter into that rest, lest any man fall after the same example of unbelief. For the word of God is quick, and powerful, and sharper than any twoedged sword, piercing even to the dividing asunder of soul and spirit, and of the joints and marrow, and is a discerner of the thoughts and intents of the heart. (Heb 4:8-12)

We enter God's rest by faith. That is the only work which is not self effort, because we have the faith of God. We thus declare to ourselves: "I have entered His rest." The striving part comes as a result of our circumstances and soul emotions contesting our confession. So we stand firm in our belief disregarding any outer storms which attempt to make us sway in our inner conviction. This striving will ultimately transform our faith into substance.

The giants the Israelites feared when they stood on the brink of entering their promised land of rest is a type of our soul emotions and our fear of our flesh. We erroneously think that we have to fight those feelings, attractions and desires which raise their head in order to deter us from entering our promised land which is Him in us as us. At the cross He won that crucial battle and cleansed us completely from indwelling sin. There is nothing wrong with our flesh. He is our keeper! Our flesh is His means of manifesting Himself in this temporal realm, that is, "those who have seen me have seen the Father".

The word of God, Christ, who is joined one spirit to us pierces to the division of soul and spirit so that we are empowered to discern between what are soul emotions and what is our inner spirit knowing. This knowledge and enablement to discern is powerful in rejecting everything which rises against the knowledge of God, who is our rest. Jesus provided this land of rest through the cross. We already have it, and we recognize and possess our heritage through faith, and we boldly enter His rest knowing this is His good will for us.

49

A Bruised Reed

A bruised reed shall he not break, and the smoking flax shall he not quench: he shall bring forth judgment unto truth. (Isa 42:3)

God's principal concern is always human beings – the pinnacle of His creation. His idea was to gather a family of sons under His wings. To make them true sons and be partakers of His heart and His nature, which main characteristic is self-giving love for others, He had to let them go their own ways so they could develop a consciousness which could compare and contrast between the negatives and positives in this world (Luk 15:11-32).

He Himself descended to this temporal realm to partake in the human project which was finished at the cross (John 19:30). His firstborn of many sons was made perfect through what He suffered so that He could be a high priest who is not unable to sympathize with our weaknesses, but one who in every respect has been tempted as we are, yet without sin (Hebr 4:15). God in His humility walked with man on this cursed earth, so He himself could share the burden concerning the progress of man. He in fact chose of His own free will to carry the entirety of what He began when we created beings with a consciousness. His objective was that they could reach their completion in Him so that they in Him could experience that death works in them to life for others (2 Cor 4:12), that is, His sons promoted to priests.

In His heart we find unsearchable love and compassion for His beings. There is not a thing He will not do to see them return to His heavenly lap. He would rather die than see any of them perish. So that's what He did. When His love has led them to a position where their fire of self-love is quenched and everything which is left is an ember of the eternity He has put in every human's heart He very gently begins to blow on the ember until it bursts in to a flame nourished by His life. He never ceases to give or breathe His life unto His family, because that is who He is. Souls almost crushed by life's many travails He with affection and tenderness bandages with His love. He would never condemn, preach to or lay heavy burdens upon a bruised reed. The heaviest burden of them all, the law, He fulfilled

Himself so that every Human could experience His love which has no boundaries. This is His justice!

No Wants

There was a time in my Christian walk when I wanted so many things. I wanted to become a better father, better husband, more loving, more caring, less judgmental and so on. Norman Grubb calls those wants rubbish, and I agree wholeheartedly.

Those wants expressed my erroneous belief that I had to improve myself using my own willpower. I have reached the conclusion that's not the case, since I am either indwelt by sin or Christ. Since I have been given life through my faith in Jesus I am indwelt by the latter. I thus do not have an independent operating self which is designed to reflect myself, which is the illusion our soul enemy wants to perpetuate. Every one of my wants became veils which impeded me from recognizing my new union with Christ and my perfection in Him, and that I reflect Him in my human form as the perfect version of myself. This of course is the mystery of the gospel.

I also believe that God used my wants so that that illusion concerning an own independent self that had the power to improve itself could be completely shattered when I came to the end of myself. Our wants of improvement also become our idols. We fix our gaze on our goals, and are distracted from our center, which is Christ and Christ alone.

It is quite clear to me that if God accepted me into His family of sons with everything I am, I can accept myself. If I am good enough for God, I am good enough for myself. He is my keeper, it is His life that is manifested in my mortal flesh. I say as Jesus: "I can do nothing of myself." So, if God wants to better me He has to do it. I just relax with no condemnation seeing Him accomplish His works in me.

Who am I to judge myself? Christ is the judge and his verdict is: "Innocent." And if I am Christ in my form I am promoted to make righteous judgments as well, and my verdict of my existence is: "Holy, righteous, perfected son." I have literally kicked my former consciousness of sin on the ash heap. It was a burdensome nuisance which smothered my precious liberty in Him.

I also remember that I wanted to be used by Him, to yield to His will etc. Well, the truth is: I am all those things. How, you may ask. Through faith! I have practiced (He has practiced as me) to recognize Christ in me until it has become a fixed inner spirit knowledge. Our faith develops by hearing the word. That's what I have been doing the last year; immersed myself (He has immersed Himself) in teachings which edifies and encourages me to take those leaps of faith which enabled me to acknowledge everything He attained at the cross on my behalf.

Ever since I accepted Christ I have been all those things He says I am, but it has taken 17 years for Him to lead me to the understanding I now have. Every step has been carefully planned by my loving Father. I can see that in retrospect.

Perfect from Infancy to Maturity

John claims that the Christian walk is characterized by three stages; children, young men and fathers (1 John 2:13). When Jesus walked this earth he went through the common human seasons; infancy, childhood, adolescence and maturity. In every stage of his earthly life he was found without sin (Hebr 4:15).

John also asserts that we can have boldness on the day of judgment because as he (Jesus) is, so are we in this world (1 John 4:17). Moreover, the author of the epistle to the Hebrews states; "For by one offering he hath perfected forever them that are sanctified." Both verses encompass the same truth, our perfection in Christ.

In addition, John alludes to our union life – the mystery revealed – Christ in us living as us (Col 1:27), when he writes that as he is so are we. God's master plan is to regenerate man so that humanity and divinity is perfectly amalgamated into one being, which is both us and Him and where it is impossible to discern between the two. A perfect union.

Paul corroborates with John's stages when he differentiates between what kind of food the Christian is able to digest in 1 Cor 3:2; "I have fed you with milk, and not with meat: for hitherto ye were not able to bear it, neither yet now are ye able." Meat, however, is for the mature.

What we can infer from this is that Jesus' different stages in life symbolize the different stages the Christian goes through as a new creation. If Jesus was perfect from infancy to maturity it is not far stretched to assert that this also applies to our grace walk. For most believers this calls for a leap of faith.

When established in this amazing truth our entire outlook will be altered, and how we view our sisters and brothers who still are unskillful in the word of righteousness will be revolutionized. This truth empowers us as well to accept and love ourselves as perfect in Him.

This perfection concerns body, soul and spirit. We are compelled to assume that this perfection applies to all of our human entities on account of Jesus who was the son of man coming in the flesh. If we limit this perfection to only the spiritual realm we are unwittingly limiting Jesus' perfect sacrifice, and we are standing on the threshold of Gnosticism.

Faithful in All His House

Paul likens our relationship to God with a marriage. We died from our former husband, the law. Then we were resurrected to be with our true husband. The fact that our earthly marriages are a type of our heavenly union is the obvious reason why God doesn't like infidelity particularly well. One of the things the new gentile churches thus were to abstain from was sexual immorality. God is a jealous spouse because He loves us so compassionately.

In 1 Cor 7 Paul literally says that the spouses own each other. They have authority over each other's bodies. Have you considered the implications of this? It means that we as His spouses have access to and authority over everything He owns. We can relate this to what Jesus said about us being given the keys to the kingdom of Heaven, that we are commissioned to bind and loose. We perhaps see this more clearly when we remember that we are in God, and that He is in us. He owns us and we own Him. Moses knew this secret, because Hebrews 3:2 says that Moses was faithful in all His house.

How much more do we not have access to all His house under the new covenant?

There is a small detail, however, before we can take the necessary leap of faith and operate on this level effortlessly. The Holy Spirit must first have established us in a position where we never accept condemnation. As soon as we begin to assert our rights the Devil will come against us with all sorts of temptations and accusations.

But, we stand fast without the slightest condemnation, and we know the difference between a temptation and a sin. Jesus was tempted as we are. He is well acquainted with the Devil's strategies, and since Christ is in us the enemy has nothing in us. We do not fall back on self effort, which is infidelity, but stand fast in Him.

As long as we are sojourners on this earth which is under the dominion of the evil one it is his right to come against us and test us. However, God uses those encounters to further His will in us and to exercise our faith. We come out even stronger, more confident and as more than conquerors when we have defeated our adversary by the blood of the lamb and our confession.

It has become more and more clear to me that if we are to be faithful in all His house we have to be safe sons. We are created as persons. Persons can choose, but they become slaves of what they have chosen. I opted to marry, and became a slave of marriage. We choose to have children, so we are slaves of our children. I became a teacher, and that choice governs my life.

To be safe sons of God means that we have tasted darkness and we have tasted light. We know the difference between sin and righteousness. We have experienced the wretchedness of self effort, and found the surpassing excellence of rest. Project man was finished at the cross, and out of it a multitude of safe sons emerge, because they are knowers. Their experiences are the foundation for their choices, and they never again have any desire to return to the former things. They can compare and contrast, and the glory of the new marriage far supersedes the things that one day will dissolve. So they reign with Him safe in His love and secure in His keeping powers. Yes, it is all of grace! Yes, we are slaves of righteousness.

Sinless Perfection

If we are to call ourselves true fundamentalists we are forced to take into consideration and ultimately have an unwavering faith in the Biblical principle of sinless perfection. The opposite, sinful imperfection, might seem from an earthly perspective to be closer to the truth, and is thus the prevailing idea in most churches. When Jesus said: "Be you perfect as your Father is perfect" he was not kidding around. That was not a call to fervent self effort, but a statement of a soon to be actual reality for whosoever entered His kingdom through faith. It was a call not to live by sight, but to live by faith. John had the nerve to say that as He is, not was, so are we in this word. Every quality we attach to the ascended Christ is also true about us, John asserts. Life at its fullest is found in this almost absurd notion that there is nothing wrong with me, but that I am perfected through a once and for all sacrifice.

Eternal Love

God's humbleness came into display when His son was born in a stable and laid in a manger in a country occupied by alien forces. That same humbleness is manifested every day in people who have given their lives to Him and who He isn't ashamed of calling His offspring. They are sojourners on this planet which one day will be dissolved in the same manner as the consciousnesses of those who love Him are shaken until their minds can contain Him.

The mysteries of God are only conceivable to those who have given up everything with a desire to be filled by Him. In this state they discover themselves as true beings liberated from any inhibiting outer limitations. In their uniqueness there is a diversity and freshness that is captivating. In every man He makes Himself known in a distinctive way.

Our Father's main objective is to see us soar like eagles liberated from the gravity of appearances to be to free to walk boldly in faith trusting ourselves as perfect manifestations of His humble divinity. His desires are like a consuming fire and everything He has resolved according to His own free counsel will see its completion despite any evidence of the contrary.

The same consuming fire has He endowed on every son. This eternal flame scorches off self effort and any constraining illusion of independent self until the creation sighs of relief witnessing another safe son step forward confidently emanating the kind of love that words into being the Eternal Love's desires.

Everything Means Everything

God is love. It isn't something He has, it is something He is. At the outset of our walk as new creations we find it difficult to reconcile life's many facets with His love. As we grow we come to understand that we receive His love through faith, more often than as an experience. Then the Holy

Spirit establishes this as a truth in the innermost corners of our being – and His love becomes knowledge. We have all experienced that His love can also be manifested in tribulations and sufferings leading us to a deeper sense of His all encompassing love.

An undisputable fact is that as new creations we are in Christ. If we are in Christ and He is love, then we also are love, simply because His sap flows into the branches. This goes beyond feelings and appearances, because it is a spiritual truth. Let us not in this part of the account begin to contrast evil and good, because there exist no such thing in our being. In Christ we do the truth and we do what is right, which basically is being in Him and let His life flow in us.

The next step is to acknowledge that everything works together for good for those who love God. Regarding our love towards Him; this is not either a question of feelings; it is a plain fact that we love Him because He loved us first. When we strive to please Him we do not easily recognize His love; that is true. However, those who have entered His rest bask and revel in His unconditional love.

He is the one who works everything for good. His highest good is Himself. When we behold our actions, attitudes and behavior and judge them according to our perceptions of good and evil, which is a heritage from the fall, we often feel that we fall short. That is not the truth, however. The truth is that He uses everything – everything plainly means everything – to advance His good.

If we have disappointed someone, which we occasionally do, God employs that to work forth His good in that situation. Disappointments and other things which are not so pleasant have the inherent power to lead people to the end of themselves and thus solely rely on God. In other words God's love in us may cause tribulations for others so they can experience His highest good – Himself.

Seems odd, doesn't it? Not exactly what we have been previously taught. This is of course just a marred and simple illustration, but I hope it gets the point across. I am not saying now that we should dispense tribulations on others as we please, just that those things inadvertently occur, and when they do they are also an opportunity for our Father.

The conclusion is: Rest from your own seemingly failures and rest in Him. When you do the sap flows unstrained and you are everything you are, a perfect mirror of Him.

Bread And Water

After the Spirit revealed the revolutionary news to me that Christ is in me I find it immensely difficult to say that I am dry. It is an impossibility since the Everlasting water springs up inside me and lives inside me and its fresh wells soak my entire being. I find it corresponding difficult to assert that I am spiritual hungry now when the Heavenly Bread continually feeds me with its abundance inside of me.

He has been there my entire Christian walk, but it wasn't until I recognized the facts and faith became substance that I wholly could rely on Him as my sustainer. What an amazing difference this constitutes. Of course I have my bad days when my soul is in uproar, when self pity finds a crack or tiredness overwhelms me. However, those emotions do not any longer define my being in a negative way. And perhaps most importantly: I never give them the opportunity to condemn me, because the truth has become a tangible reality to me. I have come to love my emotions knowing that I am perfectly capable of expressing Him and myself through them. Emotions are an asset. They color my life.

If my soul emotions happen to bother me a quick glance at Him inside of me is all that is necessary for my soul to calm down and find rest. You see, I am fearfully and wonderfully made. God really put an effort into the making of me, and when He was finished He smiled exclaiming: "It is very good." Recognizing His presence within me has also released this unspeakable joy which earlier just was a remote idea of something

58

unattainable in this life. So from having a Christ out there, the illusion, to have a Christ in here makes all the difference in the universe.

I AM

Repentance is simply acknowledging that "I can't" and say to God "you can". There is no condemnation for those who can't. Those who still attempt to live the Christian life are, however, in a precarious position and are an easy prey to condemnation and the activities of the flesh. The flesh says: "I can". That is idolatry.

Faith, however, says: "I am willing to let You". It opens up to His ability and His resources. The Christian life isn't a self-improvement program. It is supernatural and divine. This involves a process where the regenerated man increasingly recognizes and embraces Christ's activity in him.

Repentance is to recognize that God's Kingdom is within. Repentance leads to faith, and faith investigates its inheritance. It is not an inheritance hidden in a dim future, but it is here and now. What is this inheritance? Isn't it a fearfully and wonderfully made me who is dressed in Christ? So I joyfully investigate the new creation.

When I let go and let Him I walk in the Spirit free and bold knowing I am a son of the Most High. Paradoxally, I have now found myself and I fill the whole picture with everything I am.

The **"I can"** identity's "I" and "my" are filthy rags!
The **"I can't"** identity's "I" and "my" are glorious!

The One Jesus Loves

Now there was leaning on Jesus' bosom one of his disciples, whom Jesus loved. (John 13:23)

This is perhaps one of the most beautiful pictures portrayed in the New Testament of intimacy between Savior and disciple. John writes of himself that he was loved by Jesus. Not that the others were less loved, but John had understood that he was accepted and loved by his master. Can you imagine yourself resting your head on God's bosom?

Do you have this inner knowing that you are esteemed by God, and that He delights in you? Do you yearn to rest your head on His shoulder or bosom (which also means heart)? Can you picture yourself being embraced by the tender love of the One who has created everything?

Doesn't this image make you feel special? Doesn't it make you bold in His presence? John could be bold with Jesus because He knew he was loved. No need to pretend when you are together with a person that loves you unconditionally!

Did you know that John is derived from Hebrew and means God is gracious?

Evolvement

In his first epistle John introduces something not found elsewhere in the Bible. He suggests that the Christian walk can be divided into three separate periods, where each period has some common characteristics. I have been pondering this lately and what I am now to pen down is not an exhaustive exposition on the subject, merely some initial thoughts.

The little child knows his sins are forgiven. He is not yet, however, secured in God's grace and has a limited understanding of the mystery of the gospel, that is, Christ's abiding presence in him. The child is an easy prey for condemnation, and is apt to judge himself and others based on behavior. He prefers fixed boundaries and finds security in a predictable religion.

The child usually wants to have its will and God have mercy on those who is so audacious that they shake their outlook and their predictable world. Children prefer predictability and strict boundaries. They prefer to divide things in good and evil.

The young man has overcome the evil one. He has disclosed the devil's devices and is secure in his identity. He is strong because he has discovered the surpassing power of the One who abides in him. The adolescent is well settled in God's grace and he is beginning to make righteous judgments in accordance with the light he has been given.

Otherwise the young men are like most other adolescents. They almost invariably know better than those who are older and more mature than them. Full of plans and energy they embark on any project they think will glorify God.

The father, who knows Him who has been from the beginning, has delved into this mystery we call love. He knows God is limitless and unsearchable. He has found that God operates outside any preconceived boxes. Daily his mind is stretched, because the Spirit is leading him further and further from the trodden paths. The father is completely secure in God's love. The fact that he is loved is a fixed inner knowledge. He is not dependent on feelings, sensations or experiences to feel loved even though he appreciates those moments of intimacy.

What does it mean that the father knows Him who has been from the beginning? God is love and thus love is the origin of everything. It is a love that far surpasses any human understanding, so the father has undressed himself of those inhibiting thought patterns which attempt to understand God intellectually. God is Spirit and can hence only be recognized in a realm where words cannot by any means make justice to God's person or ways. The father has abandoned any earthly ways, and his soul is utterly captivated by the beauty of the Eternal one.

For the father any illusion about separation has been dissolved and he is well established in his union with God. His will is fused with God's will and he confidently obeys his heart knowing he can do nothing of himself and is thus secure in his own I. Paradoxes do not scare him. On the contrary he is intrigued by the freedom those almost preposterous inconsistent ideas offer.

Others envy him his freedom to express himself without any inhibitions. In the same manner as God the father is preoccupied with one thing only and that is life and life in abundance.

When He Lingers

Now Jesus loved Martha, and her sister, and Lazarus. When he had heard therefore that he was sick, he abode two days still in the same place where he was. (John 11:5-6)

This is really an oddity. I thought that if you loved someone you would hurry to their rescue. But, no! Not Jesus. He follows a different timetable. I for sure would have preferred that He swiftly came to my salvage when I was in trouble. I don't know how you are wired, but if I learn that someone is in dire need I do not postpone my involvement or aid for two days because I love that person.

Anyway, there are some great lessons in those two brief sentences. If Jesus doesn't come to your rescue immediately it doesn't mean that He has abandoned you or that He doesn't love you. On the contrary, if He lingers it is because He loves you dearly and because He has a miracle up His sleeve.

Your deliverance will come in His perfect timing and when it comes it is going to render you in utter awe. In the meantime He asks you to trust Him and make your bed, that is, make yourself comfortable in your transient "hell". When Jesus raised Lazarus from the death many turned to Jesus and believed in Him. So, your troubles aren't perhaps so often about you, but as a beloved child of the Most High you are His conduit for bringing life and repentance, that is, a change of mind regarding God to many.

I ask you to never assume that Jesus doesn't love you when you face your dreaded darkest hours, because He does. In fact, He goes through those seasons as you. He intimately knows your thoughts. He cries with you, and your heart's sorrows break His heart. If you listen carefully you will hear Him in your heart saying: "I have gone through this before. I know how it is and I know how to deal with it. If you put your trust in me you will see that I carry you through everything. And it is my responsibility to glorify you and myself through it all. So, rest in me."

"He loves you not only because you are here, but also you are here because He loved you into existence" (Malcolm Smith)

We Are the Objects of Agape

The Greek word for love is Eros. It has the same meaning as the English word love. It denotes the kind of love that responds to beauty and harmony. Eros loves those who deserve its affection. It strives towards the highest and best, and everything which doesn't match its standards fall short of its devotion. This love is repulsed by what it find ugly and of less quality.

Eros is driven by this desire to fulfill its own cravings and to own the objects of its love. It enjoys the hunt and finds it thrilling to conquer, and it reduces what it desires to mere objects or things to possess. To contrast and compare and come out at the top makes Eros the kind of love that the Pharisees displayed when they were basking in the affirmation from their peers.

Eros thinks that if religious duties are well performed it will earn God's favor. Its worth is based on its accomplishments and it cannot fathom that God will stretch out His hand to tax-collectors, prostitutes, thieves and homosexuals. Eros likes to boast of its beauty and that it is blessed because of its good deeds. This kind of love is on shaky ground, because whenever it witnesses God's kindness towards those it consider unworthy its system of values is challenged and its response is often religious anger.

Agape is a Greek word that seldom was used in the days the New Testament was written. It was a word with a rather general meaning, but it was this word the Holy Spirit exclusively used in the New Testament and gave it His own meaning and definition. Agape arises spontaneously from the heart of God, and it loves both the ugly and the unworthy. Agape shows no partiality. It loves unconditionally both the prodigal son and the self-righteous son.

Agape seeks out that what is in disharmony with God. It even embraces its enemies, those who would like to see it dead. This is the kind of love who loves the spiritual unattractive. It isn't awakened by religious deeds or good works. Because God is love agape originates in who He is, not in us being lovable. So His love seeks us out with compassion and with no strings attached. Its highest desire is to see the objects of its love liberated and set in freedom. It asks of nothing in return and it finds its fulfillment in those who humbly receives it with gratitude because they have nothing to offer.

Agape stirs the depths of the hearts of those who recognize it and welcome it. This is the kind of love that turns hearts of stone into hearts of flesh. Agape can never be deserved so those who trust in its Source are standing on firm ground. Agape is scandalous in its affections and thus rejected by the religious minded who thinks in terms of Eros. There are a couple of other properties which we can attribute to Agape that are almost outrageous; it never feels ashamed over its recipients and it never turns its head in disgust when they fail miserably.

You and I are the objects of Agape!

Turning to Jesus

Often we find that people associate particular emotions or resolve into the term repentance. Brokenness, remorse, guilt, shame, rededication and self-introspection are often demanded if a person's repentance is to be assessed as genuine. However, if this is the model we apply we inevitably are confronted with a couple of episodes recorded in the scriptures which challenge our understanding.

Eros love demands that a person does something to earn its approval and forgiveness. However, God operates on a completely different level through His unconditional Agape love. Thus He is eagerly waiting for the prodigal son to return, even running to meet and embrace Him. This son erroneously thought that his Father had nothing more than Eros to offer him, so before he went home he had planned what he would tell his Father when he returned including all the necessary phrases and resolves. But, the Father wouldn't listen to any of it on account of His agape love.

This parable tells us that repentance is simply turning to Jesus. If we put anything else into this expression we demonstrate our predilection towards a legalistic system of reward and punishment. We are also confronted with the thief on the cross who simply turned to Jesus and was saved. He had nothing to show for himself except faith in God's grace.

Often God's grace and generosity is too much for the human mind to grasp. We don't like that God makes it so easy for persons to be reconciled to Him. We prefer to think that they must put in an effort to better themselves first or that they display all the emotions we associate with repentance so that they can deserve His kindness.

We are designed to be spirit people. When Eve and Adam fell the only thing we had left was our flesh. We knew somehow that something was missing. Man began thus searching for the meaning of life outside his original design. As a flesh person man exalted wisdom, intellect, progress and even sex as the meaning of their existence. They missed the goal, which is sin.

The meaning of life is simply to walk in a relationship with the Creator. Anything less than that is missing the target. Repentance is thus to turn from our futile and void pursuit of what seems to the flesh as the ultimate meaning of life and turn to God. The thief on the cross did exactly that, turned to Jesus and was saved. Moreover, we are continually saved by His ascended life, and we continue our process of repentance after we are saved by dismissing our misguided ideas concerning God's agape love and replace them with the stupendous truth.

And he said unto Jesus, Lord, remember me when thou comest into thy kingdom. And Jesus said unto him, Verily I say unto thee, Today shalt thou be with me in paradise. (Luke 23:42-43)

Well Watered

In that day the LORD with his sore and great and strong sword shall punish leviathan the piercing serpent, even leviathan that crooked serpent; and he shall slay the dragon that is in the sea.

In that day sing ye unto her, A vineyard of red wine.

I the LORD do keep it; I will water it every moment: lest any hurt it, I will keep it night and day.

Fury is not in me: who would set the briers and thorns against me in battle? I would go through them, I would burn them together.

Or let him take hold of my strength, that he may make peace with me; and he shall make peace with me. (Isa 27:1-5)

One of the words the Bible uses to define our human condition is vessels. A vessel contains something. It either contains sin or it contains righteousness. Sin found its dwelling place in man after the fall, and we thus understand that sin and the devil are equal terms in the scripture. Every person who accepts Christ is cleansed from that former indweller. When it comes to the serpent God is merciless and kills him so that there is no risk seeing him returning to the sea, that is, our spirits.

When this passage refers to "that day" it refers to the dispensation which came into effect after the cross. We who are regenerated are the fine vineyard, where He is the vine and we are the branches abiding in Him producing His fruit. A different translation says: "...every moment I water it." According to my calculations every moment is every new now. He who is the great I AM lives in the now, and He sustains us every moment of our being. In fact He more than sustains it, He keeps it well watered so it never lacks, but has an abundance of every good thing.

I believe it is not too far stretched to view the sea as a type of our consciousnesses. We all know how we are composed of conscious torrents and subconscious torrents. When everything is well our seas are calm. However, when the gale is coming our way the waves rise. He who lived in our private sea is dead. He loved to whip up the sea. Our Father who now reigns over the sea secures us that we are safe with Him.

"I am not angry. I care", He says. A multitude of Christians still believe that God is angry with them. Carefully they watch every step they take, they are obsessed with confession in order to mitigate an angry God. This passage clearly states that God isn't angry with us. His anger is directed towards the indwelling sin who has usurped His dwelling place. The fact is that He has never been angry with us. The indwelling sin, however, has been well aware of His fury towards it, and of course this has been imprinted on our consciousnesses. The Spirit is now thus convincing us about our righteousness and His love, which slowly but surely will liberate us from the bondage of fear.

What are thistles and thorn bushes, we might ask. Man's main occupation since the fall has been to build his own righteousness. Whether that has been by observing the law or attempting to erect a sense of worth through other means is of less interest. However, it is a well ingrained habit, so those thorns are self-effort. Our Father lovingly pulls them out by letting us come to end of ourselves, to the point where we give up and accept that He is our life.

Why would God, who is joined one spirit with us and who lives in us be angry with us, that is, Himself? He never makes any mistakes, He is perfect and He indwells us. To assert that God is angry with us is the same as saying that He is angry with Himself. That is a ludicrous idea. In Him we find a good and whole life. That is our destiny. This life is expressed as us. That is our work, that is the pinnacle of faith; self-expression!

The Greatest Miracle

There is a great and magnificent miracle that many find difficult to believe is possible. It is not healing. Even pagans believe that their witchdoctor through some magical rite can heal them. It is not life after death. Even New Age adherents believe there is an afterlife. I don't think I am wrong if I assert that the miracle most people find almost impossible to believe in is that someone can love them unconditionally.

Receiving Like a Child

For many years I found it terribly difficult to receive gifts. There was a perpetual sense of unworthiness and even a nagging feeling that I had to do something to earn them which made this basic task very difficult. This was not a problem when I was a child. However, as my self-consciousness grew and as life's many disappointments and blows came in rapid succession my innocence and natural ability to spontaneously receive crumbled.

Paul said in Romans 5:17 "...much more they which receive abundance of grace and of the gift of righteousness shall reign in life by one, Jesus Christ." And Jesus told us that we had to turn and become like small children to enter the kingdom of God. This explains quite succinctly why my first season as a believer was such a "disaster".

From we were infants our parents gave us everything pertaining to life. Utterly helpless we were completely dependent on our parent's care and gifts. We were experts on receiving. The idea that we had to merit their care didn't exist. Moreover, we often demanded their attention and care without giving that issue a second thought. Naturally we moved in a realm of receiving and taking, because their possessions were evidently also ours.

There are some possessions which God owns that He has a strong desire to give His children. Those are: Abundance of grace, the gift of righteousness and the kingdom. He says that when we receive those gifts we will reign in life. Jesus told us that if we don't have the mindset of a child we will reject the gifts on account of our inclination to think in terms of rewards. However, the law guarantees us that if we attempt to earn His gifts we are doomed to fail.

It wasn't that God loved me less when I in my self-righteous fervor tried to deserve His gifts and favor. The simple and sad fact was that I was unable to recognize and accept His love, because I firmly believed I had to earn His approval and gifts. Of course that marked my life. If you believe you are serving a demanding and angry God, you become angry and demanding. That is definitely not reigning in life.

Man's most important and basic faculty is to receive. Unable to receive we are distorted versions of our original design, and a distorted version will ultimately flounder. Jesus met and cared for a special group of people who found it very easy to receive His love and acceptance. They were the outcasts of society; prostitutes, leprous, tax collectors and their likes. So I guess those of us who think we are something in our own eyes are those who find it most difficult to receive His unconditional love.

I have learned the hard way to receive from my Father. His love had to break me first before I could turn and become like a little child. I am immensely grateful that His grace and love found the task of leading this man to repentance worth the effort. Well, He had made up His mind before the foundation of the earth when He proclaimed: "I will!" And His determined "I will" is like an unquenchable flood so my ability to receive is continually improving.

Friends

But thou, Israel, art my servant, Jacob whom I have chosen, the seed of Abraham my friend. (Isa 41:8)

I am a descendant of Abraham. There is no doubt in my mind that this is true and an uncontestable fact. I am Abraham's offspring, because I share the faith of Abraham. In other words I am God's first choice. I am of perfect quality. God has fearfully and wonderfully made me, and when He had finished the task He said: "It is very good!" As a new creation there is nothing wrong with me. I am perfected through one offering.

God calls Abraham His good friend. Hold that thought for a second! The creator of the universe calls a created human being His good friend. Do you think that you are worse off than Abraham? Your Heavenly Papa calls you His good friend as well. What a majestic thought that is! For many years I thought that few would like to be my friend. I perceived myself as boring, rather dull and not particularly exciting to be around. Those signals I received from the surroundings seemed to verify my suspicions. My negative self perception became increasingly entrenched in my mind and as I grew older, and my conduct reflected my poor self image.

It wasn't until Jesus picked me up that I began to loosen up, notably when He began to show me how much He appreciated my unique being. He didn't have any problems with me being an introvert. In fact He found my thought processes very intriguing. I aroused His curiosity. He plainly told me that He wanted to be my friend. I truly appreciate His friendship, because He is so supportive. He is never disappointed in me or angry with me. Even though I sometimes can be very quiet He respects my moods. He is never importunate. We have a lot in common. We read the same books and enjoy the same kind of music.

His loving friendship has untangled a lot of knots and I am thus flourishing like never before. He has even showed me some sides and talents that my Father has endowed me with that I wasn't aware of and which discovery has enriched my life considerably. I am far from being boring. On the contrary, I am a very colorful and exciting person to be with.

Dressed in Fine Linen

"And to her was granted that she should be arrayed in fine linen, clean and white: for the fine linen is the righteous deeds of the saints." (Rev 19:8)

How many righteous deeds are you able to perform during a day? I must admit I have lost count. They simply flow quite effortlessly and natural from me, so I do not give them much thought. There was a time, though, when I with great eagerness kept a track record of my sins, or to be more precise, my imaginary sins. Ignorantly, I wasn't aware of the fact that I was dressed in fine linen.

I hope you don't mind if I share a secret with you: I have relocated from Mount Sinai. I have some vivid memories from that place, though. It was in those days that my consciousness was filled with thunder and lightning. My thoughts were billowing with clouds and smoke so that I couldn't see clearly. And it was when I was there that I had this crippling fear of God which rendered me in a state of mind where I seldom dared to approach Him. I preferred to keep a distance, because as long as the commandments and sin dominated my outlook I had this terrible feeling of always falling short before my Father. I thus thought He was terribly disappointed in me.

I now live on Mount Zion, a mountain renowned for its stunning scenery. It is a joyful and peaceful place. Another fascinating quality with this mountain is that it is always sunny here. Clouds and smoke are completely absent, so the view is never obstructed by a deprecating consciousness of sin. With this new clarity in sight I am empowered to distinguish the real me. Moreover, I am always close with God. Even though I do not always feel His presence I know we are connected in a unique and indissoluble way.

Mount Zion is my guarantee that I am as righteous as Jesus. I see that clearly now. God has not dressed me in fine linen to cover my filthy, dirty self. When God does something He does it thoroughly and not half heartedly. I am clothed in righteous deeds as a sign of my new status; clean through and through. I didn't earn my righteousness. It was a gift which I received and fully embraced when I switched mountains.

Do you think I live differently now when I know that I am righteous? Of course I do! All of us live according to how we think. To linger on Mount Sinai as new creation is like being a former convict who voluntarily prefer incarceration and bondage to liberty and a life as a free citizen with all the rights that entails. The quality of life soars exponentially when you are a free citizen of Mount Zion.

Shouting From the House Tops

You have most certainly noticed how the Spirit spurs you on to take new steps of faith. He begins His mission by quietly whispering some new and profound truths in your ear. Either are those truths too good to be true or they are beyond your mental ability, because they involves accepting something which might seem as a complete paradox, or those things He whispers are so beyond our material realm that we do not have any points of reference. What we thought was our secure ground is now dissolving under our feet.

However, the Spirit is patient so He continues to unravel those places where the knots are so tight that they impede our ability to process any new ideas. In an odd way we can sense how He is working in us until suddenly the dam bursts and our faith becomes substance and the things He initially whispered to us now have become ours and in our mind it feels as though we now are shouting those magnificent truths from the house tops. What a wonderful release that is.

A reasonable question now is; why all this? The truth is that we have been deceived. When we accepted Christ a revolutionary thing happened. We became new creations. Jesus says about us: "…for they are not of the world any more than I am of the world." The deceiver does not want us to know this magnificent truth. The enemy thus makes any effort to make us stay earthbound in our outlook and entices us to build our identity upon what we can see.

However, appearances fall far short of conveying who we really are in the spiritual realm which is our true home. The eternal truth about us far supersedes any identity we might have acquired during our years on this planet. The Spirit hence convicts us about our innocence and that we are righteous. Our true identity is not dependent on our efforts to become something we desire to be in this temporal realm. It is not based on works, occupation, education or social position. If we are to be safe sons of God our identity has to be based on something unshakeable, and that is Christ. Thus John in his first epistle observes that as He (Christ) is so are we in this world.

We embrace our true identity by faith, but faith is not faith before it has become substance, that is, we know that we know. The Holy Spirit is our helper in this very important process. When the light is fully lit in our understanding those beautiful truths He initially whispered to us are now palpable realities in our lives, and in our consciousnesses these amazing, from an earthly perspective almost preposterous truths, are shouted from the house tops.

What a Blissful Mystery

I get this warm fuzzy feeling inside whenever I am contemplating God's love. His plan is so wonderfully majestic that I am rendered in utter awe. Who would have imagined that His plan of salvation would involve that the kingdom would be established in hearts of flesh? That heaven is inside every believer where Christ has found an eternal resting place? I am quieted by the fact that He in His mysterious humbleness has chosen to make Himself manifest in human flesh. Every single cell in my body is sustained by His life.

My entire being leaps with joy when He tells me that I am not of this world, that I am a partaker of divine nature and that I am destined to spend an eternity with Him. His love desired my existence into being, and I am now a part of that triune flow that has existed from before the foundation of the world. How could it be otherwise? He will always remain faithful, because He cannot disown Himself. He has sworn an oath regarding His relation to me. Since He could not find anyone greater than Himself, He made the oath with Himself. He will always remain faithful to His oath, because He is unchangeable and cannot lie!

I am thinking about the mystery of the cross where I went into Christ in His death and disappeared for suddenly being resurrected in Him as a new creation with an entire different genealogy from the one I had. I am new through and through. Who would have imagined? In His love He is fussing around making sure that I know who I am in Him. That is His greatest delight to establish His beloved son in who he is. His heart almost bursts with pride when He beholds me. He is boasting unconstrained of me wherever He goes in the Heavenly realms. Could it be otherwise? After all, I am His offspring!

Gain His Glory

"Whereunto he called you by our gospel, to the obtaining of the glory of our Lord Jesus Christ." (2 The 2:14)

I spent some time one day pondering on this verse. My initial conclusion was that I didn't like the word "may" (it says *may obtain His glory* in a different translation) in the context particularly well. It was thus natural to make an attempt at finding out what this "may" was pertaining to. Would we gain the glory of the Lord Jesus Christ after we had left this temporal world? I soon rejected this idea, because God is operating in the now. The now is His prime concern in His dealings with His precious children.

My second approach was to reflect on whether this "may" perhaps was pertaining to some condition we have to fulfill in order to see the manifestation of the promise. For instance if we walk in the Spirit and not the flesh then we will most certainly gain the glory, I reasoned. However, that seemed as a very shaky foundation for the fulfillment of a promise. With all these thoughts swirling in my mind I got into the car in order to pick up our daughter. I put on some music and relaxed to the enchanting rhythms and terrific guitar work of Paradise Lost.

When I turned the first curve a new thought hit me with a compelling force. What if this "may" was pertaining to God's dreams and will from before the foundation of the earth? What if His desire always has been to see a succession of sons who share in the glory of His firstborn son here and now? However, in order that they "may" gain this glory He had to sanctify them first. And so He did through one offering for sins. I am without a shadow of doubt sanctified in Christ, and if I am sanctified I have also gained the glory of my Lord Jesus Christ. Since I am unable to see my glory I trust that what God says about me is the absolute truth. I find it quite futile to discuss matters that He of His own free counsel has decided, notably when those matters are to my benefit.

Those we encounter in this temporal realm can, however, detect our glory. I assume what Paul observed covers this remarkable thing: "Now thanks be unto God, which always causeth us to triumph in Christ, and maketh manifest the savour of his knowledge by us in every place. For we are unto God a sweet savour of Christ, in them that are saved, and in them that perish: To the one we are the savour of death unto death; and to the other the savour of life unto life. And who is sufficient for these things?" (2. Cor 2:14-16)

A River of Love

Jesus said that we are no more of this world than He is of the world. There is perhaps thus no wonder that we now and then receive severe beatings from a system that do not recognize us, and is inclined towards hating us in the same manner as it didn't welcome Jesus' light. We will seldom receive the glory and the honor that are due to us when we are sojourners in this temporal realm. There is only one who fully knows us and whose eyes run to and fro throughout the whole earth, to give strong support to those whose heart is blameless toward him (2 Chron 16:9).

It is thus imperative that we carry a correct image of God in our hearts. When we receive our blows we need a safe haven where we can find strength for our souls; a place of comfort and approval. Where can we turn to if we believe that even our Father is against us and disappointed in us? If we direct our gaze towards the world for consolation the likelihood of new disappointments are quite high. If we don't dare to approach our loving Father because we carry a distorted image of Him in our hearts we have no place to turn.

Unfortunately, there is many a sincere believer who does not think that the verse cited above applies to him, because He hasn't embraced or heard in a faith infusing way the tremendous good news about his new standing with God. Our hearts are blameless toward Him. He has chosen us in him (Christ) before the foundation of the world, that we should be holy and blameless before him (Eph 1:4). That we are blameless is an uncontestable fact!

God's love is like a river that always seeks the downtrodden, that what is little. Water has the unique quality that it with great certainty finds a way to the lowest parts, where the pain is excruciating and the cravings for love are most desperate. Its fresh and life giving water envelops completely its objects. Even though its torrents are rejected it continues to flow because it is the sustainer of life. That is its nature. It cannot cease from flowing.

My friend, if you have had a tough day there is One whose heart is fully with you, who utter those blissful soothing words that saturate your whole being and who picks you up so you can find rest in His bosom. His love is your destiny, your final destination. His love is your home.

A Glorious Temple

Salomon had been commissioned the glorious task of erecting a temple to God. His father David had purchased and gathered the necessary building materials. It took seven years to complete this magnificent temple (1 Kings 6:38). The last thing they did was to bring into the temple all the things his father had dedicated to the building; silver, gold and all the vessels.

The building lacked one thing though; the presence of God. When the ark was carried into the building and the priests came out of the Holy Place a cloud filled the house of the Lord. The priests could not stand to minister because of the glory of the Lord.

In the new covenant we know that God doesn't dwell in buildings. He fills every temple, in other words, every man into whom the ark, that is, Christ has entered. From our spirit, the Holy Place, His glory permeates and fills the entire temple, our entire being. Every corner and hidden nook is packed with Him. He is the sole and only occupant of this tremendous temple. There is room for no one other than Him. Thus the whole building is perfectly holy; spirit, soul and body.

The fact that the priests could not stand to minister due to His glorious presence symbolizes the end of the old dispensation of annual sacrifices which perpetuated a conscience of sin. Something far better would come into effect. A once and for all sacrifice has been carried out which states that I am crucified with Christ: nevertheless I live, yet not I, but Christ lives in me (Gal 2:20).

In 1 Kings 9:3 God makes a most astonishing promise: "I have hallowed this house, which thou hast built, to put my name there for ever; and mine eyes and mine heart shall be there perpetually." There were, however, some conditions that needed to be met for the promise to stand firm. However, as we all know; Jesus Christ has fulfilled every condition on our behalf so that we with boldness can continue our walk knowing that our salvation is eternally secured!

Jesus IS Come in the Flesh

Hereby know ye the Spirit of God: Every spirit that confesseth that Jesus Christ is come in the flesh is of God: And every spirit that confesseth not that Jesus Christ is come in the flesh is not of God: and this is that spirit of antichrist, whereof ye have heard that it should come; and even now already is it in the world. (1 John 4:3-4)

Most other translations say that Jesus has come in the flesh. That gives us associations to a time two thousand years ago. Most can agree on that there lived a man in that period of time named Jesus. The dispute mainly revolves around whether He was the savior of the world or not. That's not the issue in question in this article.

What John throws out here in his epistle as it is rendered in the King James version is dynamite. Jesus is come in flesh means here and now. The thought is so staggering that we have to pitch our arms in utter amazement. Jesus here and now? Where? There exists only one answer. Jesus is come in the flesh in every believer.

This is so overwhelming and have so huge implications for how we are to view ourselves that the enemy will go to great lengths to avoid that this is common knowledge in the Christian community. However, what John asserts squares perfectly up with some of Paul's observations, notably Col 1:27 and Gal 2:20.

The spirit of antichrist is in opposition to the fact that Christ is come in the flesh, just as it opposed Jesus in His time. Notably, the Pharisees and the Scribes couldn't fathom that God had found a dwelling place in common human flesh. In some of their rather fierce encounters with Jesus He said that the god of this world was their father. That puts things in their right perspective and we understand what the source of their antagonism was.

Jesus was just an ordinary man, a carpenter from Nazareth, but He was God's son. The scriptures repeatedly call us sons of God in spite of our commonness. Despite the fact that Jesus was a common man He knew who He was and where He came from. And what an ego He had. "I am the way.." "I am here.." "I have come..." "I will...". Simultaneously He said: "I can do nothing of my own!" Our false humility is effectively exposed by how He viewed Himself and how He interacted with the world.

Since Christ is come in the flesh and has joined Himself to common human beings like you and me it is about time we raise our heads and acknowledge who we are in God and assert our egos because in our union with God they are reflections of Him. As Jesus we can do nothing of our selves. Spontaneously we do what God does and we recognize this tremendous fact through faith. This is the secret, the mystery of the gospel which Jesus intimately knew and which lifted Him out of His commonness to live in accordance with His original design as a son of the Most High.

The Sabbath Rest

"And Jesus saith unto him, The foxes have holes, and the birds of the air have nests; but the Son of man hath not where to lay his head." (Matt 8:20)

Jesus was searching for a resting place, a specific day when He could rest from all His works, that is, a Sabbath rest for His divine being. We are that day, that Sabbath, where our savior can lay His head and rest. Simultaneously, He is our Sabbath rest, because we are in Him and He is in us. This is a profound mystery; how we are joined together in one spirit and how both the human and the divine find rest when they are amalgamated and become one in spirit. This is what the entire creation is eagerly anticipating; the Sabbath day when it will be liberated and enter its perfect rest when reconciliation is consummated.

Complete in Him

The Holy Spirit has done a tremendous work in my life and has convincingly convicted me about my righteousness. There is not a doubt in my mind that God has taken possession of me. He fills me completely and in the same manner as Jesus came in the flesh I have come in the flesh to manifest my lovingly Father. The fact that Jesus came in flesh simply denotes that He was a visible expression of the invisible God through His soul and body faculties. Born by the Spirit His flesh was holy and perfect. My flesh isn't found wanting either, because the same power that dwelled in Christ now dwells in me.

There was a season in my earthly life when my flesh was filled with sin and it followed the prince of the power of the air. The problem wasn't my flesh, but who the occupant was. My soul and body are fearfully and wonderfully made designed by my Father to mirror Him, and when He had finished making me He observed that it was very good. When the false spirit was cast out I was restored to my original purposes and design. To accuse my flesh of being of inferior quality or that it has some deadly flaws is in reality saying that God did a poor job when He regenerated me and that I have to fill in what is lacking. That is not the gospel.

Sin is no longer an issue in my life. John says that I cannot sin, and I embrace this by faith. However, I almost daily face temptations. Not to sin, but to return to a mindset where I reject who I am in Him, to doubt that I am a beloved son and that God every second of the day with minutely concern works forth His will in my life. I am tempted to fix my gaze downwards instead of upwards. I am tempted to let worries and problems smother me in their intensity. I am thus tempted to be carnal minded as a substitute to the one I really am, and that is a partaker of divine nature with the mind of Christ. Jesus faced the same temptations as I do. In the wilderness the enemy repeatedly challenged Jesus with "If you are the son of God….."

Jesus was tempted to demean His divinity in all the three parts which constituted His being, that is, spirit, soul and body. In other words both His spirit and His flesh were under attack, but Jesus with great perseverance refused to let the enemy belittle who He was in God. If Jesus had given in to the pressure He would have been in Eve's position and concluded like she did that there was something lacking in how He was created and hence had to become like God in His own powers. Through this encounter Jesus established forever who He was in God. Jesus was driven into the wilderness by the Spirit. God had purposed His temptation. In the same manner He purposes our temptations so that we can be settled and fixed in who we are in Him.

The Great Debtor

I am debtor both to the Greeks, and to the Barbarians; both to the wise, and to the unwise. (Rom 1:14)

When we walked according to the spirit of error we considered everyone and everything to be our debtors. When we gave, it was usually with an expectation that our generosity would be rewarded or reciprocated. We were creditors. Why would Paul consider himself a debtor to peoples he never had met or had had any dealings with? The answer is love. Paul was completely soaked with God's love.

We humans have never quite figured out why God loves us so cordially. His love has an ethereal dimension which is very unfamiliar to the unregenerate man. He, the creator of everything, expresses His love as He was a debtor to every one of us. Hence He gives and gives abundantly. It is His nature. That is His way of life. We are receivers and that is the intention of our design. We are thus conduits through which the quality of His love will be spontaneously expressed.

John asserts that as He (Christ) is, so are we in this world. It plainly denotes that there are no "ought to be" left in our lives. We are everything we are supposed to be. When we are saved we begin to share with others this wonderful new life which is burning with an eternal flame in our hearts. We have become debtors to those God sends in our way. And we find that it isn't a burden, because we have become unconditional love in action. We love, because He loved us first.

Twice the New Testament exclaims that God cannot lie. A lie is an obvious sign of self-seeking love. The motivations behind a lie can vary, but a liar is ultimately seeking his own ends. God cannot lie, and thus His love will always seek the benefit of others, that is, Christ being formed in every man. This is the most amazing gift there is because it is God giving Himself as an eternal gift to those who accept Him.

A debtor is always in need of a creditor in order to find fulfillment and gratification for His existence. Hence Paul repeatedly in Romans 5 make statements such as "the free gift", "the gift of God", "the gift by grace", "the gift unto justification of life" and "abundance of grace." Our Father's eternal desire has always been to share His quality of life with the pinnacle of His creation. Hence a love song of indescribable beauty swings back and forth with an irresistible harmony in the heavenly realm. If you listen with your spiritual ears you can hear it singing joyfully in your heart.

The Holiest of Holies

Jesus said: "I do only what I see my Father is doing". This is the pinnacle of faith expressed by the One who was the first example of a succession of sons who would soon emerge born of the Spirit. But why and how could Jesus make such a statement? Did He have a second voice in His mind that determined every step He took, or did His observation refer to something else? Let's start our investigation with some reflections on the Old Testament tabernacle.

The priest could only enter the holiest of holies in the tabernacle once a year to make atonement for the people's sin. He did so trembling and with great fear. The rest of the year the innermost room of the tabernacle was separated from the holy place in the tabernacle by a veil, and no man could enter the holiest of holies without risking his life. There had to be an atonement for sin before anyone could enter that place. It was in the holy place and the outer courtyard that the priests ministered during the rest of the year.

If we are to be able to tie the aforementioned regarding the tabernacle with Jesus' observation we have to leave the physical world with its appearances and move to a different level. The outer rooms in the tabernacle thus represent separation in man's consciousnesses. Man living apart from God. That God is somewhere out there apart from us. When Jesus died at the cross the veil was torn apart and everyone borne by the Spirit in the same manner as Jesus was could now enter the holiest of holies where there is no separation in our consciousnesses. God and man one, no longer apart. The truth is that they had never been apart, but this was how man perceived his existence. To enter this sacred place also signifies that sin is done away with once and for all. If not no man could have entered the holiest of holies.

Jesus was the second Adam and borne by the Spirit. He had unlimited access to the holiest of holies in His consciousness. Jesus saw no separation, that is, that God was apart from Him. Union with God was an established fact in His consciousness. He hence boldly could walk in the Spirit knowing that He was a manifestation of His Father. Everything He did was thus the Father finding an expression through the Son. So whatever the Son did the Father did. Jesus could behold His life and see His Father operating spontaneously as Him, because there was no separation in His consciousness. It is on this backdrop that we understand why Jesus could say: "I do only what I see what my Father is doing." "Only" doesn't refer to that the Father put limitations on His life, but that He could see union only.

On the cross Jesus cried out: "'My God, my God, *why have you forsaken me?*" This is the cry in every human heart which hasn't been born by the Spirit and entered the holiest of holiest. Of course, God never forsook His son in this darkest hour, but Jesus had to leave the holiest of holies in His consciousness when He became sin for us and thus experienced the sensation of apartness that has been the prevailing mindset in every man so that He through His sacrifice could open a way into the holiest of holies for every man borne by the Spirit.

We cannot understand Spiritual realities without guidance and revelation from the Spirit. The physical tabernacle in the Old Testament was just a shadow of the things to come. In the new covenant the tabernacle pertains to our consciousness, that is, how we perceive our existence in relation to God. If you still believe that God is apart from you you still haven't entered the holiest of holiest even though the way in is cleared for you. It is in the holiest of holies that the liberty of the Spirit finds an expression, that we become a law in ourselves apart from the Old Testament law, that we live without condemnation and are established in the union and can say as Jesus: "I do only what I see my Father is doing"; the pinnacle of faith.

A Hypothetical Paradox

For if we sin wilfully after that we have received the knowledge of the truth, there remaineth no more sacrifice for sins, But a certain fearful looking for of judgment and fiery indignation, which shall devour the adversaries. But a certain fearful looking for of judgment and fiery indignation, which shall devour the adversaries. But a certain fearful looking for of judgment and fiery indignation, which shall devour the adversaries. For we know him that hath said, Vengeance belongeth unto me, I will recompense, saith the Lord. And again, The Lord shall judge his people. It is a fearful thing to fall into the hands of the living God. (Hebr 10:26-31)

The author of the Hebrews has gone into great detail explaining the prevalence of the New Covenant compared with old. He has gone to great lengths assuring the believer about his new standing with God, and he even asserts that a child of God does not need to have any consciousness of sin because of a once and for all sacrifice. He even cites God saying: "I will remember their sins and their lawless deeds no more." Then he writes this passage which has caused the opposite effect of security in many a believer. We even get the impression that the author is contradicting himself.

The profundity of this verse is that it confirms us as persons with the ability to choose, we are something far more than mere automats. The if-clause makes this passage a hypothetic discussion of impossibilities – a paradox. He in a way says that if you were in a position to choose Christ you are also in a position to reject Him even though you have tasted His goodness and mercy. The paradox is that if you again is returning to sin, which is the spirit of error, there must be a change of spirits again. However, that is impossible, because it was God who shut the door to the ark when everyone had entered.

The author of the epistle has through various examples shown how the believer has been transformed from an outer person to an inner person. An inner person has the law written in his heart and he spontaneously expresses it as the fruit of the Spirit. For such a person there is no law, and moreover, he has no consciousness of sin and he is safe. He has found peace with God in his Spirit. A return to being an outer person arouses sin consciousness, he has no longer peace with God, he will again behold God as a God of wrath and he has rejected Christ's sacrifice. This hypothetical person's faith has thus become void. Another point is that Jesus has made a once and for all sacrifice. Therefore there remain no more sacrifices for sin.

How did man become a self conscious person? What is a self conscious person? When are infants awakened to that they are persons? Isn't it when they come to realize that they can choose? God placed two kinds of trees in the middle of the Garden. Eve thus had a choice and it was when she exercised her ability to choose she acquired the awareness of being a person and not a mere automat. She made, as we all know, the wrong choice. However, Eve tasted and discovered the opposites in life. Without her discovery we would not have been in a position to choose, and most importantly; choose Christ.

Our conclusion must be that the author in this passage continues his exposition of the good news, and here in particular he confirms the authentic personhood of a believer. It is crucial if we are to be true witnesses of Christ that we are completely safe in our relation to our Father, and that we are firmly established as true persons. Free and safe sons, just as Jesus demonstrated, are in a position to be intercessors for a needy world.

Born in a Manger

My saviour was borne in a manger in the midst of manure and the pervasive smell of animals. There was no room for Him in the hostels, and there never is. It was in my derelict building amongst ugliness and foul smells His life again found a place to be manifested. Not many saw it and perhaps I was the one who saw it the least. Little did I know that the saviour of the nations was born in me. It wasn't until God revealed that Christ was formed in me that my inner eye was opened and I could see this miracle taking place in this most unlikely place. Christ come in the flesh again defying any religious ideas of God.

Christ has grown in wisdom and stature until one day He stepped forward as a mature full grown man. That is, my consciousness has in increasingly measure been enabled by the Spirit to behold this mystery. This evolvement hasn't been something that has gone from worse to better, or from less to more, but from glory to glory. For Him to be fully formed it has been necessary to oppose and rebuke religiosity and legalism in this nation. However, compassion and love has flowed like a wild river when His companion has failed miserably or faced temptations and afflictions which have almost worn him completely out. All this have been of God so that this manger could be transformed into a glorious castle. When darkness has surrounded the building and it has been attacked from every perceivable angle God has turned on the lamp and I have recognized that He was there even in the fiercest of battles, and with a vehemence unbeknownst to man He has slain every enemy which has raised its head against the knowledge of God.

He is the all in all. Even when the pile of dirt has been so huge it has obstructed every view from my limited vantage point He has used it for His redemptive purposes. He is greater than everything and humble enough to identify with nothingness so that He can be recognized as the all in all. Who is like Him? His rest is so encompassing that it far transcends the notion of having died to the law. He is the rest. He is the all encompassing sufficiency. True rest can only be found when He is acknowledged as the one who fills everything and purposes everything after His counsel to the redemption of His creation. Every moment self-consciousness finds a crack in the mind He is diminished and oneness seems like a distant reality. Nevertheless, He is there working forth His magnificent will so that the abundance of life can flow unimpeded to His glory. To be in Christ means no condemnation, that is, it is I, yet not I, but Christ who lives in me. I am found as I am in Him in every now, because that's where He is.

It Is Finished

Jesus cried out: "It is finished", but in God's mind it had been finished from before the foundation of the world when the lamb was slain. In our linear perception of time it was finished two thousand years ago. From God's perspective it is and has been forever eternally finished. He has never doubted the outcome, He has never been caught off guard by the enemy's strategies. The Lord has watched over our coming and going both now and forevermore.

Every now, every moment of our lives it is finished. There is nothing we can add or deduct. Despite this glorious fact many a sincere believer is deceived into thinking that there is something lacking in his salvation, that his sanctification is deficient. There are legions of "shoulds", "ought tos" and "must nots" that cause him to howl inwardly with pain. His seemingly failures throw him to the ground again and again and there is nothing he can do about it.

Utterly helpless he walks among the tombs not recognizing they represent everything He has died from. Desperately he shackles himself hoping he can control his cravings and coveting. It is only Jesus' "it is finished" that reverberates trough the universe that can set him truly free and make him proclaim through the whole city how much God has done for him.

Reassurance

And hereby we know that we are of the truth, and shall assure our hearts before him. For if our heart condemn us, God is greater than our heart, and knoweth all things. Beloved, if our heart condemn us not, then have we confidence toward God. And whatsoever we ask, we receive of him, because we keep his commandments, and do those things that are pleasing in his sight. And this is his commandment, That we should believe on the name of his Son Jesus Christ, and love one another, as he gave us commandment. And he that keepeth his commandments dwelleth in him, and he in him. And hereby we know that he abideth in us, by the Spirit which he hath given us. (1 John 3:19-24)

Condemnation robs us from confidence, boldness, faith and joy. However, God is greater than our heart, plainly because He has given us a new one (Ez 36:26). In His magnificent generosity He calls the new heart ours and it is. Every one of us knows deep down within that we are a unique person.

Every time our Father beholds our heart He sees a reflection of Himself. John further on says He knows everything, so there are obviously things that we do not yet see or understand, but those things are clearly so very much to our advantage that there is no need to experience any condemnation, which by the way is a residue from having eaten too much fruit from the three of good and evil.

God's objective is to have us standing in His glorious presence with confidence, which synonyms are self-assurance, poise, coolness and buoyancy. Now a wonderful promise follows: "Whatever we ask we receive from Him". It should be clear that there are a lot of things we do not have to ask for, things He has already freely given us and which He wants us to understand He has given us (1 Cor 2:12):

• But to him that worketh not, but believeth on him that justifieth the ungodly, his faith is counted for righteousness. (Rom 4:5)

• Therefore as by the offence of one judgment came upon all men to condemnation; even so by the righteousness of one the free gift came upon all men unto justification of life. (Rom 5:18)

• In the body of his flesh through death, to present you holy and unblameable and unreproveable in his sight. (Col 1:22)

• Therefore being justified by faith, we have peace with God through our Lord Jesus Christ. (Rom 5:1)

• But we all, with open face beholding as in a glass the glory of the Lord, are changed into the same image from glory to glory, even as by the Spirit of the Lord. (2 Cor 3:18)

• Blessed is the man to whom the Lord will not impute sin. (Rom 4:8)

• But he that is joined unto the Lord is one spirit (with Him). (1 Cor 6:17)

• To whom God would make known what is the riches of the glory of this mystery among the Gentiles; which is Christ in you, the hope of glory. (Col 1:27)

• For ye are all the children of God by faith in Christ Jesus. (Gal 3:26)

Our Father is immensely preoccupied with our daily living, what we call the small things in life. He loves to show us His ability to make Himself manifest in every detail of our lives. One of my favorites is to ask Him find a parking place, and He always find one not too far from the elevator. Ask God about those things that concern your daily life, because it is here that He also lives and exists in us. He has found a dwelling place within us, manifesting Himself in human flesh in regular daily human routines. This is indeed a great mystery.

We receive because we keep His commandments, and they are very simple: Believe in His son and love one another. Our work is to believe in Him who He has sent (John 6: 28-29). Furthermore, He has done for us all of our works (Isa 26:12). When we rest from all our works we find that the Spirit within neither slumbers nor sleeps (Psalm 121:4). His activity within is a well of joy and life. Love is just as easy; we love because He loved us first. It is a perpetual out flowing of His love.

John's aim with these verses is to assure us that we are of the truth and reassure our hearts before our Father. It is as God says through him: "Be still and know I am God."

By the Grace of God

Paul says a most wonderful thing to the Corinthians: "By the grace of God I am what I am." The words resonate with acceptance of his being. In a way he says that God has formed and molded him by His grace so that he is everything he is meant to be. Nothing less, nothing more. To the Galatians the same Paul says: "He who had set me apart before I was born, and who called me by his grace."

Paul had reached a level of understanding where he saw God only. We all know how Paul was a Pharisee of the strictest order and how he persecuted the church before he met Jesus on the road to Damascus. Despite his rather gloomy past Paul asserted that God had even been there and orchestrated his life and through that season prepared him for his glorious task of bringing the word of reconciliation to the Gentiles.

To the Romans Paul observed: "But where sin abounded, grace did much more abound." God is glorified and proves his adequacy in turning what in the temporal realm seems like a hopeless case into something most stunning in His kingdom. Paul is the perfect example, and somehow he knew he was. The past, the negative became the backdrop for the positive, the glory of God's grace which shines so radiantly when it is contrasted with the gloom.

You are not any worse off than Paul. God has set you apart from before the foundation of the universe to be who you are. You have been through different seasons which have prepared you for your high calling of being a son of the Creator of everything. Many a time you have faced things which others have meant for evil, but which God has meant for good. You are not the result of some random influences. Your loving Father has been there all the time hidden in persons and circumstances which have led you to your present glory. By the grace of God you are who and what you are!

A Natural Life

The Christian life is both natural and supernatural. By natural we mean that it is a natural outflow of life. Immediately this natural outflow is inhibited by outer laws it ceases being natural. If you dam a river, which otherwise quite naturally would have flowed through the landscape expressing itself in wild torrents down a mountainside or running just slowly and majestic through a valley, it has ceased being natural. Its inherent life is quenched by the erected barriers constructed by unyielding cement. In the same manner outer laws will inhibit the natural outflow of the Spirit's life in a Christian.

Everything that does not stem from inner life, that is, a position of being will quench the Spirit.

We might call this trust in our inner life, that we in fact are in a glorious union with the resurrected and ascended Christ and that He is in fact expressing Himself as us, faith. Faith viewed from this side is a state where we just are. In this almost unconscious state of merely being we have found our life again in Christ, where it is has been hidden as a contingency ever since God decided to see Himself mirrored in a succession of sons.

It is supernatural because we are not of this world. We are sojourners in this temporal realm until this age has reached its consummation. In God we have access to resources which are completely alien to the unregenerate man. Seated in the Heavenly places with Christ we express ourselves both in the natural and the spiritual world.

We refuse to again subject ourselves to any outer law whether its name is "ought to" or "ought not to". Perhaps the most subtle of them is that we have to yield more. This particular law hinges on a severe misconception, because when we accepted Christ God completely took possession of us. It is not possible to yield more than that. The Spirit is preoccupied with enlightening the eyes of our hearts so that we in increasingly measure can know the hope to which He has called us, the riches of his glorious inheritance in the saints and his incomparably great power for us who believe.

Eternal Security

The marriage between man and woman is a shadow or type of the union we have with God which came into effect in the instant we accepted Christ. God doesn't like divorces in the natural, because that ruins the image of the far superior union He has entered with the regenerated man. Thus Jesus says; "Let no man separate what God has joined together." However, in the Old Covenant under Moses the Israelites were allowed to give a certificate of divorce on account of their hard hearts. This is very important, because God hasn't a hard heart. He is love. He would thus never separate himself from, that is, divorce those who are in a union with Him. Even when we are a faithless He is faithful.

God has such a tremendous respect for the marriage that He wouldn't release us from our marriage to the law, indwelling sin and our union with Satan before we died. The instant we accepted Christ we went into His cross and died with Him. Now, we are free to marry another, and that person is God. When God swore His covenant oath, remember that marriage is a covenant agreed between two equal partners, He had no one greater by whom to swear, He hence swore by Himself that He would never leave us or forsake us. We played no part in the setting up of that covenant. He is the sole guarantor that the covenant conditions will be met. That is our eternal security!

Many say that sin can cause us to lose our salvation. That is impossible, because it was because of sin that He saved us. We were helpless slaves under its dominion. In our newness of life we are dead to sin, but alive to God in Christ Jesus. Sin is a power, a spiritual power which found a dwelling place in man when man was deceived by Satan. That power is forever cast out. We are free from its demands. We might commit sins, but we are every instant cleansed by the blood. Sin can never cause us to lose our salvation, because it was because of sin that He came to our rescue.

One of the images the Scriptures use to describe our being is vessels. A vessel is filled with something. That is its natural faculty. God created man from the dust of the ground and breathed into his nostrils and man became a living being. Then man was put in the Garden. In the garden there were many trees. Our attention is drawn to the Tree of Life which was in the middle of the garden. The tree of prominence. In addition there was the tree to knowledge of good and evil.

The tree of life represents Christ, because later on we learn that if man had taken of the tree of life he would have lived forever. Christ is eternal life. Two trees, two possible unions. As a vessel man is created to be filled with something, and He chose the wrong filling. When we have accepted Christ the former union is dissolved and we are now filled with the tree of life, which is eternal life. To assert that a borne again person can lose his salvation is in effect saying that God will permit that that person again is filled with the spirit who is at work in those who are disobedient. That is an impossibility. That would be to annul the cross. That would be to deride Jesus finished work.

Noah's ark is a wonderful type of Christ. Every man and animal that entered the Ark was saved and protected from the flood. In the same manner every regenerated man is in Christ. In Him we are safe and protected forever and ever. It wasn't Adam who shut the door when everyone had entered the ark. "And they that went in, went in male and female of all flesh, as God had commanded him: and the LORD shut him in." (Gen 7:16). God was their guarantee! He personally sealed the Ark. No one is greater than God and no one can remove God's seal. His firm resolve is that not a single soul that has found shelter in Christ will ever be separated from Him.

Paul said: "For I am persuaded, that neither death, nor life, nor angels, nor principalities, nor powers, nor things present, nor things to come. Nor height, nor depth, nor any other creature, shall be able to separate us from the love of God, which is in Christ Jesus our Lord." (Rom 8: 38-39) Nothing means nothing!

Safe Sons

"For the earnest expectation of the creature waiteth for the manifestation of the sons of God." (Rom 8:19)

A son of the most High is a safe son. He has through the fall tasted the wretchedness of being a child of the spirit of error. He knows firsthand the emptiness and nothingness of a life where everything is defined by good or evil. A true son has experienced the futility of erecting his own righteousness. His attempts of observing the law failed miserably. He knows firsthand how appearances are just illusions of a world in which he is now just a sojourner. God's sons are well acquainted with sorrow and tribulations. They have been under the curse and have vivid memories of its misery. After they have tasted God's grace and received an unwavering faith in God's goodness and love the enticement of returning again to a state of slavery holds no appeal to them whatsoever.

A true son has encountered the negatives and the positives of this world. He has allowed the positives to swallow up the negatives. In the same manner as when God said; "Let there be light" and the light swallowed up darkness, the son has let the light of Christ shine in his life by accepting Him through faith. He has become a see-througher who recognizes that God is all in all, and that God's self-for-others-love sole and only objective is to gather everything in Christ through mercy and love. A safe son knows that it has all been necessary. Without it he could never have reached the pinnacle of the creation; personhood. A consciousness of being a person with choices. The son sees clearly that when he received Christ a change of reigning spirits occurred. The sin deity is replaced by God, and it is now God's life which is being manifested through him.

A true son has given up his life, and thus found life. A quality of life hitherto unknown to him, but he embraces it with everything he is, because he has acquired a profound understanding through everything he has experienced; this is true life – this is what he originally was meant to be. As every man reaches true sonship a breath of relief goes through the creation as it waits for its final liberation from its bondage to decay and will be brought into the glorious freedom of the children of God. As everything will be gathered in Christ, everything will be gathered in His sisters and brothers as well to the glory of God. God's generosity and love is boundless. He freely shares Christ's inheritance with His offspring – the seed of Abraham.

The Key of Knowledge

In one of Jesus many encounters with the Pharisees and lawyers He exclaims: " Woe unto you, lawyers! for ye have taken away the key of knowledge: ye entered not in yourselves, and them that were entering in ye hindered." (Luke 11:52) How had they taken away the key of knowledge? Jesus said about them: "For you load people with burdens hard to bear." Outer laws become a veil that obstructs people from acquiring knowledge, according to Jesus.

What kind of knowledge is Jesus talking about? I believe Paul answers that question in 2 Cor 13:5; "Know ye not your own selves, how that Jesus Christ is in you?" The context is that also the Corinthians had had their share of false apostles visiting their church proclaiming a different Jesus. The result of this Paul says would be that their thoughts would be led astray from a sincere and pure devotion to Christ.

Outer laws impede the regenerated man from recognizing the mystery which makes the new life new through and through, namely that Christ lives in us. We have unlimited access to all His resources when it comes to living the abundant life. Living by outer laws leads to the misunderstanding that Jesus gives us power, love and everything else we think we lack in order to have a victorious life.

However, Jesus does not give us those things! Simply because He is everything we need, so that when we recognize His abiding we understand we are everything He is. That's the liberating secret! That is knowledge. And the key that unlocks the mystery is grace; pure undefiled grace!

Free at Last

"Think not that I am come to destroy the law, or the prophets: I am not come to destroy, but to fulfil. For verily I say unto you, Till heaven and earth pass, one jot or one tittle shall in no wise pass from the law, till all be fulfilled. (Matt 5:17-18)

When Jesus said that without Him we can do nothing, we hear Him, but we don't believe Him. No wonder then that so much of what we hear or read more or less have a call to some sort of self-effort. In many instances this call is so subtle that if we haven't exercised our faculty to make spiritual judgments we might easily fall prey to those calls, and as a result condemnation isn't far from knocking on our door.

The route God takes us in order to disclose our utter helplessness is through Romans 7. In Romans 6 we experience our freed self. We have moved from the dominion of darkness to God's kingdom, and now we are ready to live the Christian life. Motivated to please our loving Father we approach the task with energy and high hopes. However, we soon discover, just like Paul, that we do not understand our actions. We are unable to do what we want, and we do what we hate.

It is in this state of wretchedness that God reveals Christ in us and we move into Romans 8 where we begin to live the victorious union life where we finally have found ourselves in Christ. Here we discover that the One who has fulfilled the Law and the prophets lives and moves as us. The outer laws which we in our once former ignorance with great fervor attempted to obey we find are fulfilled in us by Christ. Therefore there is no condemnation for those who are in Christ Jesus!

The righteous requirements of the law are now fully met in us, and finally we can accept ourselves just as God has accepted us. Concepts such as good and evil are beginning to be dissolved and lose their grip in our consciousnesses, and what we have left is right being, that is, the tree of life. So, here I am with a profound understanding of that my original design is fully restored. This is the truth that liberates.

The Obedience of Faith

Twice in Romans Paul refers to something he calls the obedience of faith. The scriptures tell us that Christ became sin for us and died for us. Through His once and for all sacrifice we are justified, righteous, sanctified, holy, saints, pure, dead, resurrected and ascended. In Him we go from glory to glory. Briefly told, that is the content of our faith.

Faith to salvation is quite easy compared to all the other things we hold as true. Faith isn't easy, that is why Paul talks about this obedience of faith. Daily we are faced by inconsistencies. We lose our temper, our thoughts are a different story and we struggle with a variety of temptations. It seems like we are rendered in the middle of a battle zone, where our faith is challenged from many angles.

In order to understand this more thoroughly we have to investigate our death and compare it with Jesus' death. Jesus death was an all encompassing death. All three parts of Him saw death. When He was in the grave He completely had given up His life. Since He had emptied Himself of His rights before He entered this temporal realm He couldn't raise Himself from death. Thus the Spirit raised Jesus from the grave and gave Him back His life (Rom 8:11).

We who are still alive have experienced a spiritual death. We died in Christ and were also raised by the Spirit. However, our soul and body haven't yet tasted death like the death Jesus experienced. Jesus is thus both perfected and untemptable there He is sitting at the right hand of the Father. We, however, are perfected and temptable. That's the difference! So we are pulled, pushed and tempted in this evil world. But, why?

Where do you go when you are sick? You go to the doctor. He is a specialist. He has been trained with the objective of dealing with people's ailments. Well, this world needs spiritual specialists as well; people who are well trained in the obedience of faith. So, we are educated through those pulls, influences and temptations to become spiritual experts who can aid those who are struggling towards a settled obedience of faith.

We feel fear, we have reactions, there are doubts and there is unbelief. We experience rejection, hurt, anger and a variety of feelings. Through them we discover our humanity. Our job isn't to purify all those things. What we do, however, is refusing to accept any condemnation on account of our humanity. Obedience of faith means that despite any appearances we stand grounded in the truth which often seems to contradict the actual realities. We are hence equipped to bring about the obedience of faith for the sake of His name among all the nations (Rom 1:5).

Virgin Birth

Elizabeth exclaimed in a loud voice to Mary: "Blessed is she who has believed that what the Lord has said to her will be accomplished!" Jesus, the son of man, was conceived through a juxtaposition of faith and the miraculous work of the Spirit. Every day new sons are conceived through faith and the power of the Spirit. Man believes and the Spirit creates. The virgin birth is repeated every time the seed of a new son is conceived by the overshadowing of the Spirit in accordance with that person's faith. Every new birth is preceded by God exclaiming over the person: "Greetings, you who are highly favored! The Lord is with you."

Faith is Being

The word fact can refer to verified information about past or present circumstances or events which are presented as objective reality. In science, it means a provable concept. (Wikipedia)

The author of the Hebrews plainly states that faith is the substance of things hoped for, the evidence of things not seen, in other words; faith is facts. To establish something as a fact demands evidences. When we are to advance a case we have to present evidences that are convincing and which withstand scrutinizing. A fact thus becomes a provable concept. We won't always find that others share our conviction, but, nevertheless, to us what we know is a reality.

In our personal processes towards faith God convincingly builds His case so that we can stand firm whatever circumstances we encounter. Facts are not feelings. If we are to base our faith on feelings we are that proverbial wave of the sea that is driven and tossed by the wind.

We are not either to assert that we have faith when the thing we have is partial faith. One of the few men in the Bible that admitted he had a partial faith was the father of the son who was possessed by an evil spirit. He cried out in despair: "I believe, help my unbelief." Jesus honored his honesty and imparted to him what he lacked, and cast out the spirit from his son.

There are seasons in our lives when we feel that we are light-years from God. We are completely unable to sense His presence. As a consequence we begin to doubt our conversion, and we are inclined to think that our union with God is a hollow concept from a gullible era in our lives. However, it is during those periods that God proves that our union with Him is not grounded on feelings, but that it is an undisputable fact, so that we can know who we are in Him in despite of what comes against us.

For thou wilt light my candle: the LORD my God will enlighten my darkness. (Psalm 18:28) God is the One who imparts to us that illumination which transforms partial faith into unwavering faith. Faith is not a result of self effort. What we do, however, is continuing confessing the truth despite our circumstances with an expectant trust that God will light the lamp when we are ready to enter new level of insights.

Then we experience what John so cleverly put into words: "He that believeth on the Son of God hath the witness in himself." A witness bears testimony about the truth, the realities that are our secure foundation. This witness is in us. It fixes us in the truth. The inner witness isn't a feeling, it is an inner knowing. We just know that we know.

There are many things in our lives that are facts. I for instance know without a shadow of a doubt that I am a man. I do not have to confess on a daily basis that I am a man. I effortlessly and unconsciously look like a man, behave like a man and think like a man. For long periods of time I do not give this fact much thought. I do my things and live my life almost unaware of this reality. We can almost call this the law of facts. Every area of our lives that are founded on facts renders us in a state of being, that is, we are.

When we are so secure in our union that we just are, not giving the basis of our faith much thought so that we live our lives, do our things almost unconsciously of the reality that we are in a wonderful, life-giving union with God we have entered what I believe Jesus meant when He said that true worshippers shall worship the Father in spirit and in truth.

The Sabbath Rest II

The author of the Hebrews repeatedly expounds on a rest which the regenerated man is encouraged to enter. The one who enters God's rest has ceased from His own works, as God did from His. This is in other words a rest which is the consequence of realizing that we can do nothing without Christ. The book of Revelation contains many images which when they are spiritually understood draws a picture of the battle that takes place in our consciousnesses when the Spirit does His gracious work in illuminating our minds so that we are put in a position where we disclose this lie or illusion that we are an independent self. What we discover as the Spirit's work proceeds in us is that God has taken wholly possession of us and that we live our lives in Christ and thus are His visible expressions in this realm. During this process when we discover the liberating truth of our true being we are in increasing measure revealed as the sons of God.

However, what the Spirit revealed to me is that there is an even higher level of rest which He calls the Sabbath Rest. In a glimpse I saw how everything in this world is used by God for His redemptive purposes. Absolutely everything that occurs in this universe He can turn and use for His good purposes. Nothing of what happens comes as a surprise to Him, He who is the great all in all. Then the Spirit showed me that this also applies to my life. There is nothing in my life which He cannot use for His redemptive purposes regarding my existence, and He can further on advance His redemptive purposes for others through me despite what I perceive as failures and weaknesses which I believe have the opposite effect. Everything works together for good for those who love Him, Paul says. The full effect of this insight is that my soul can find a rest which is not of this world, because He is so much greater than what I do or not do. I do not mentally understand this, that is, how He works forth His will and good purposes through both my positives and negatives. It is too great for me to grasp. However, it is on this backdrop that I can embrace my humanity as a right humanity in Him.

A couple of days later as I questioned these things the Spirit drew my attention to what happened at the cross. An event wrapped up in utter darkness. But, out of it a great light was borne. Then I saw my soul and my mind and the utter darkness they sometimes are filled with. Then He asked me: "If I could turn Jesus' death into life and joy for many how much more then can I not create light and life out of your seasons of darkness?"

You Can Do Nothing Without Me

I am afraid I again have to return to a specific thing Jesus said and which has been reverberating through my mind with increasingly insistency the last couple of days. He said as recorded in John 15:5: ".....for without me ye can do nothing."

I have always read this verse as: "without me you can do nothing good." The context of this verse is obviously that when we abide in Him we bring forth much fruit. However, the verse doesn't state what I have read into it. The word nothing is finite, absolute. Nothing contains everything. I come to the conclusion that what Jesus said only can be wholly appreciated if our point of reference is the tree of life. I obviously have read this verse from an understanding derived from the tree of knowledge of good and evil. My human definitions of good and evil fall lifeless to the ground when my life is absorbed into the tree of life. Life far supersedes any definitions I have made in order to create some sort of order in my sometimes confusing universe. It is only through faith that the tree of life becomes my secure ground from where I can receive all the promises inherent in Christ.

Without Jesus I can do nothing. It can only imply that everything in my life is Him. I have had no problems associating what I have defined as good and what I have defined as light with Him. However, my seasons of darkness, I have attributed to myself. But, now I cannot escape that definiteness of "nothing". Everything is Him. That is the total truth. I am not an independent self. I am a container of Christ. God says a most peculiar thing in Isaiah 45:7: "I form the light, and create darkness: I make peace, and create evil: I the LORD do all these things." I believe God in this verse uses words which we can understand from our limited human perspective. However, from His perspective, everything He creates is love and light which bursts forth on account of His redemptive purposes, and His ways are thus often far outside my scope of understanding. "Nothing" hence means that in His infinite wisdom I am light and darkness as well. Since God is love and light this what I perceive as darkness evidently must be hidden light. Another one of those mysteries that is too great for me to grasp. I further on cannot fathom that what I perceive as failures is Him expressing Himself as me. But, nothing is nothing, even in this context. It strikes me how humble God is. How He is willing to risk His reputation in being associated with fragile beings as me. That humbles me.

Despite all the aforementioned I know I am a person. I somehow know that I am more than an automat. I am a unique individual with everything that entails. It is now that my mind comes to the end of itself. This is an almost insoluble paradox. We are two, yet one. I find only one solution to this. There is only one conclusion that enables me to reconcile these seemingly conflicting facts and that is: I am Christ in my form. I am slowly beginning to grasp what Paul said: "But when it pleased God, who separated me from my mother's womb, and called me by his grace, to reveal his Son in me"

(Gal 1:15). His Son has been in me from the day I was born again. During the time I with great determination did my wilderness walk He was there. When I failed most miserably He was there. When I writhed in guilt and condemnation He was there. It was when I came to the end of myself and the illusion that I am an independent self was forever shattered that my lovingly Father could reveal His Son in me.

I suddenly now become to come to terms with all the exhortations and admonitions which both Paul, Peter and the other New Testament authors found necessary to include in their writings. Since I am Christ in my form, and the virgin birth is repeated in me I have gone through all the seasons Jesus went through from infancy to maturity. It should be quite clear that when I was a spiritual child I had to be under a different regime than what is called for when I am an adult. Children needs firm boundaries and a rather strict upbringing to become responsible and mature adults, but when as they grow their parents grant them more and more liberty even though that often is a rather painful process both for the maturing person and the parents. This is the mystery: Christ is repeatedly brought to maturity in persons like you and me. I am rendered in utter awe as I am allowed to see more and more of God's plan being unfolded in my life. In retrospect I see clearly that it has all been necessary. As a loving Father He has led me through pain, tribulations, misery, great achievements and moments of intimacy and love that is beyond this world. When I have been teetering on the verge of giving up, when the issues I have faced have rendered me in a state where I have wanted to die He has been there encouraging me to take another step. He has been the perfect Father in all His dealings with me. I can only imagine how it must have hurt Him to let me go through those periods when everything was dark, but without them I would still have been in infancy. As Christ has been formed in me I have gone from glory to glory. That is His perspective and that is the truth.

Some Further Musings on "You Can Do Nothing Without Me"

Christ in me is the mystery revealed. Christ is my promised land. Through faith infused in me by my inner teacher I finally, after all those years in the wilderness, reached the same conclusion as Caleb: "And Caleb stilled the people before Moses, and said, Let us go up at once, and possess it; for we are well able to overcome it." (Num 13:30). In my understanding this "we" pertains to the union with God.

Together we have conquered the people who dwell in the land. In a joint operation we have devastated the fortified cities. By enduring fierce battles my consciousness by and by has come to terms with the overwhelming truth; He lives His abundant life in me as me. After all these years I now see clearly how I have been Christ in my form ever since I was regenerated.

Sustained by the tree of life I am a safe self. What a relief to discover that I can trust myself. God is my keeper. I am His responsibility. When I now have abandoned the illusion that I am an independent self I have consciously thrown my entire being into His arms. I trust my reactions, my feelings, my emotions and my doings as an expression of His self-for-others-love. I am not sure how this works, but I am liberated from judging by appearances and thus trust that He is the one who works in me both to *will* and to work, for his *good* pleasure in whatever form that might be expressed through me.

The Right Self

"Let us make man in our image, after our likeness", God said. Image means a representative figure, and we find that likeness carries the implication similitude which means closely resembling another, a counterpart. It was from these astounding facts that we were to derive our identity, our right self. God's self perception is impeccable. There are no shadows of self degrading notions which threaten to disturb His inner peace. Evidently, as an image of Him our self was to be based in Him and have the same quality as His.

However, when Adam ate from the wrong tree this foundation for the self was shattered. After the fall Adam's children were after his likeness. They derived their self from a spiritual dead person. As a consequence this false self molded by the god of this earth became our prominent self perception. For many years I perceived myself as grey, boring, dull, mediocre, worthless, nice and well behaved with not a dangerous or wild fiber whatsoever in my being. This was a powerful lie that colored my entire existence. This false self severely inhibited my life.

The false self that we had to toil under was a part of the curse. When we come to Christ we are under heavy influence from it. We drag this heritage with us into His kingdom erroneously believing that He is just as a hard master as our former master. We believe that condemnation, self flagellation and self deprecating thoughts are the path to pleasing our new King. Even worse, many believe that those emotions have the potential to change behavior, or provide us with what we need in order to be good.

However, God wants to give us a new name, a new self, that is, our original self when we return to His fold. God has created a diversity of sons, each reflecting Him in their uniqueness. The unsearchable riches in Christ amongst other things pertain to this multitude of expressions found in Him. God's overwhelming desire has been ever from before the foundation of the earth to restore our right self. His is willing to do whatever necessary to accomplish this goal. He love guarantees that the false self will see destruction and that the right self will slowly but surely surface so that His truth will triumph.

Before we were born we were given our right self. Hidden under the false self, which we thought were us, we have sometimes seen it shine through the veil, and we have yearned for its materialization. My friend, every thought or notion that belittles you is a remnant from this false self. It is utterly false! It is an illusion – an illusion is just cotton! Yes, your right self is almost too good to be true, but welcome it as your true image. You are everything you formerly believed you weren't! God has laid the axe to the root! As a result a multitude of true and liberated sons are revealed to His glory and great pleasure.

The God of the Hills and the Valleys

Ahab the king of Israel faced Ben-hadad the king of Syria in what would become a battle concerning whether God was the God of the hills or not. Silver, gold, wives and children are the types of the good things the God of the hills provides (1 Kings 20). The question was thus and still is: Is there a God who provides the good things in this world or are they a result of hard work or are they perhaps a consequence of random selection? God gave the Syrians into Ahab's hands and demonstrated once and for all that He is the God of the hills. That's our starting point when we come to Christ. Our inner lamb is lit and through what seems as a battle in our consciousnesses we come out with an understanding that there exists a God who loves us and gives us good things in accordance with His riches.

As me move on we inevitable will come to a new junction where another and more profound question arises. Is God also the God of the valleys? Ben-haded again musters a great multitude and goes against Ahab. This is perhaps the most difficult battle we face. Is God all in all? Will we find Him in the valleys of our lives too? The outcome of this battle is essential for our understanding of God and how He works in our lives. True liberty and the peace of mind which supersedes any outer circumstances hinge on the outcome of this battle. Ben-haded, a type of our soul enemy, thus goes against us with everything he has. The outcome is however settled: "Thus says the LORD, 'Because the Syrians have said, "And there came a man of God, and spake unto the king of Israel, and said, Thus saith the LORD, Because the Syrians have said, The LORD is God of the hills, but he is not God of the valleys, therefore will I deliver all this great multitude into thine hand, and ye shall know that I am the LORD." (1 Kings 20:28)

Even though God gives Ahab a striking victory over the enemy, Ahab doesn't kill Ben-hadad. As a consequence He is prevented from being a see-througher, a man who sees God only. When we uphold the idea that the enemy still plays a part in our lives, that he is somewhat responsible for our valley experiences we maintain this double vision which causes us unnecessary strain and unrest. God is God of both the hills and the valleys. When we with a single-eye see God only our souls find rest from this world's travails. God's objective is to lead us to a place of understanding where we never give the devil any undeserved attention and as a consequence of that attention a spot from where he can influence our lives. In our consciousnesses he is hence rendered as a toothless lion whose roars by and by becomes a distant memory. There is only one God in whom we live, move and have our being. Our Abba is in full control and that goes for every nook and cranny in our lives.

Identification

It's fascinating how the Spirit as soon as we cross the threshold to the Promised Land begins what I would call an identification process; an opening up of the mind which empowers us to identify with Jesus Christ on a level that is blasphemy to the religious minded and which would be impossible for us to handle when we were under the law. Jesus was the first and foremost of many sons. He was the last Adam, the lamb who was slain before the foundation of the earth. Only He could atone for the sins of the world through His death, and provide life and hope through His resurrection and ascension. That was His exclusive ministry. Hence He is the first and foremost.

As a Son of God Jesus could utter unprecedented things such as: "I do only what my Father does", a statement that outraged the Jews since it implied an oneness with God that was unheard of at that time. It is imperative that we understand that Jesus didn't merely come to share in our humanity in order to save us. He also came as an example of us, so that we after He had accomplished His mission could share the same boldness as He displayed regarding our union with God.

So when the Spirit nudges you and challenges you to say as Jesus: "I do only what my Father does" you are in the midst of your own personal identification process. Of course, that leap of faith isn't an easy one, but it is an essential one if we are to enter this peace of God, which transcends all understanding, and which will guard our hearts and our minds in Christ Jesus. Our greatest fear is perhaps that when we get such an idea in our lap we are in danger of being led astray.

If Jesus harbored any such fears we don't know. What we know, however, is that He was tempted in the same manner as we are. It is quite clear that if He had such doubts He conquered them by the Spirit and became fixed in this truth. It is also evident that He could make such statements because He was born of the Spirit! The Spirit of truth! The Spirit of error had nothing in Jesus, thus He could completely trust those inner promptings swelling up in Him knowing who the source was. Born by the Spirit we are also sons of God, governed by the same Spirit of truth who leads us perfectly towards maturity.

When we have taken our leap of faith and dare to make the same confession as Jesus did, there comes a day when this truth becomes an inner reality. Oneness with God is no longer theory, it becomes experimental, an integral part of our lives. As our consciousnesses expand to contain this tremendous reality we unfold our wings of liberty and like the eagle unstrained surge upwards on the warm winds of love trusting this sensation as the ultimate reality; a return to our original design as illuminated persons who know the difference between captivity and liberty.

Claims

One of the many stunning claims Jesus made was: "Those who have seen me has seen the Father." Jesus claimed He was the visible expression of

God. He further said: "If you had known Me you had known my Father." Moreover; "I come from Him and He has sent me here."

Those are bold statements! I assume you are well aware of that they are valid for you too? Born of the Spirit you come from God sent here as a witness about Him. Those who have seen you have seen the Father. As was the case for Jesus, the likelihood that the world recognizes you as a visible expression of God is rather small.

The religious will say about you as they did about the crowd who followed Jesus: "They, who know nothing about the law, is damned anyway." The legalists will further mock you and say: "Look where you will – you won't find any prophet coming from Galilee." Galilee is your hometown, my friend.

You are God's visible glory! We are stunned by how God empties Himself again and again in order to be found in humans like you and me. However, that was the original plan when God created Adam in His likeness, a shadow of Himself, if you like. You are restored to your original design and thus an outshining of His glory.

Those who know you know the Father. This is simply too much for our mind to grasp. It transcends understanding. The Spirit, however, convicts us about the truth and our faith irrevocably becomes substance. Appearances easily deflect our appropriating of this all encompassing identification with our Father. However, faith supersedes any appearance so that faith becomes our reality as the Spirit does His work in us.

Please acknowledge that you are His glory and an image of Him regardless of circumstances. If He was willing to be found in a manger when Jesus was born, He is willing to be found in your life's circumstances no matter how grim. You are His beloved daughter or son. Don't let condemnation which is a product of appearances rob you from your confidence before Him and heritage in Him.

True Fasting

One of the words the scriptures use in order to cast some light on our human existence is vessel or a container. I have had some problems with this manner of describing our humanity. However, I have come to learn that this is a wonderful description if properly understood. Most of us appreciate that words just are shadows of how things really are. They are not the thing itself. To be called a container thus merely covers one side of the complexity of our being. The vessel analogy is very valuable and liberating due to the fact that it alludes to a thing that cannot fill itself with the help of its own frail powers.

To assert that a container can fill itself is indeed a ludicrous contradiction. A glass cannot fill itself. Someone outside and greater than the glass pour the liquid into it. However, we are vessels which have an inclination towards wanting to fill ourselves. That's perhaps the whole point with the vessel analogy. Man embarks on mission impossible and is repeatedly frustrated by his efforts. The law is carefully designed to disclose this fact and to reveal our nothingness as containers.

Legalistic ministries encourage believers to fill themselves with good deeds, right behavior, a successful prayer life, love and all the other things we associate with being a Christian. Since we haven't fully understood in what way that we are fearfully and wonderfully created we rededicate ourselves to God again and again and promise to do better with His help. Of course, this is a sure path to failure. In fact every attempt to live according to outer regulations is an attempt to fill oneself. There is only one solution to our dilemma; give up, rest, simply live and let Christ fill us with Himself. We are created to contain someone, to be filled by someone and that someone is Christ.

A vital point in this regard is that when we were born again He filled us with Himself. We are already filled, but we do not know it yet. What really happens when we attempt to live the Christian life is that we perpetuate an illusion of separation, that we have a life of our own when the opposite is the actual reality. Hence Christ is revealed in us when we come to the end of our self efforts. Finally, our true standing begins to seep into our consciousnesses and the redemption we have been craving for isn't a far off reality anymore.

Herein lies the magnificent liberty Jesus promised His disciples. When we discover that He is our life we cease to struggle towards an unattainable goal, and we acknowledge that every moment of failure is a valuable reminder of our nothingness. We are now in a position where we can accept ourselves with everything we are and leave it completely to Him to perfect us in our perfection in us in His time.

If we examine fasting in this light it dawns upon us that fasting is not a physical discipline, but a Spiritual discipline. True fasting is to abstain from any self effort. It is to cease from observing the law or any other outer regulation. It is abandoning the idea that we can fill ourselves with right attitudes, thinking and behavior. It is vacating trying to forcefully cultivate any fruit on this human tree by what we think are cleverly devised methods. The moment we realize this tremendously liberating reality we begin to eat. Our food and drink is Christ. He is the only food we will ever need. He is the one that fills up our spiritual stomachs.

The Inner Garden

One evening not long ago the Spirit suddenly said to me with a smile: "Adam was placed in the garden." He didn't have to say more. My curiosity was aroused, which He of course was well aware of. Day after day I pondered what He meant by those six each by them self rather innocent words. In human terms I might occasionally come out as quite clever. However, when it comes to spiritual things I am more or less brain-dead. So I simply couldn't fathom what He meant. When I came to the end of my own reasoning I began to ask if He could be so courteous to reveal His little secret to me. I thought it fair that if He had said A He also should say B. Despite several requests He remained quiet. However, He has taught me over the years to be patient knowing that He will answer in His time, which I of course counted on in this case as well.

Today I asked again wondering if He was ready to share His wisdom with me. It is perhaps more precise to assume that He lingered until I was ready. This is what He said: "Now the garden is placed in you." Interesting, don't you think? The first Adam was placed in the garden. That is an outer thing in the same manner as the law is an outer thing. Well, if the garden is in me, everything is now internalized. I am in other words a law in myself. Spontaneously and effortlessly I now meet the standards of the law since they are an integral part of my new nature. If I am not mistaken He also added: "In the outer garden there were two trees. In the inner garden there is only one tree; the tree of life." Since there is only one tree, a type of Christ, I cannot go wrong. It is utterly impossible for me to repeat Adam's mistake. I think we can safely and without being in the risk of exaggerating call this eternal security.

Water Separated from Water

When the waters were separated in Genesis 1 the material realm with its qualities was separated from the infinite and eternal spiritual realm. Time, space and distance became prominent realities for a fallen mankind. We perceived ourselves mainly as temporal beings in a temporal realm. Thus death became an enemy, because in a limited temporal realm death denotes an inevitable end.

We were like those proverbial fishes that only know their environment as a three dimensional world of water. Only when the fish sees the light penetrate the surface of its limited world it gets an idea of something beyond its experiences. Or if someone or something ripples the calm surface of the water the fish might come to understand that there is something which it cannot explain on the other side of what it thought was the border of its limited world.

In a finite world everything can be measured, gauged and counted according to the laws of this realm. A Christian keeps score on his sins and his good deeds since he has this faulty notion that the laws of his well known universe also are applicable to the spiritual realm. However, even though he lives in a temporal world he is not of it. He belongs to the waters above the expanse where everything is eternal and infinite. Counting and assessing are completely at odds with a unlimited spiritual world. How are we to count or judge in an infinite eternal dimension? It becomes utterly meaningless. It is impossible. Hence, as Paul stated, we no longer judge according to the flesh.

A new and better covenant is in effect where all those things that we formerly put our trust in are history. They are obsolete. Something better has been revealed through Jesus Christ. The Spirit patiently transfers our consciousnesses from a limited worldview to an eternal sphere where everything must be judged in accordance with this reality, that is, it must be spiritually discerned.

As an eternal infinite being we no longer are subject to the laws of this world as we know it. How are we to assess our lives in this wonderful realm where everything there is, is an eternal now? Since God's infinite love is encapsulated in every now we encounter, we are liberated beings in an infinite dimension. Everything is merged into this now where we just are. Thus nothing is counted against us. It is utterly impossible to count or keep any scores. That is why there is no condemnation in this realm where life originates and flows as an eternal river of love.

The god of this world operates within the confines of the limited realm. He counts, judges and assesses in accordance with the laws which are operative in a three dimensional world. Every believer who hasn't abandoned this world's moralistic and ethic sentiments is thus easily deceived and influenced by his lies. His weapons of condemnation are only effective in relation to a consciousness that is stuck in appearances.

The Spirit is rippling the surface of our known world so that we by faith can take the leap and penetrate the expanse and enter the waters above where we come to know who we truly are as citizens of two worlds. The material world is truly good when it is amalgamated with the truth from above.

Nothing is a Waste

After Mary surprisingly turned up and anointed Jesus with expensive ointment as recorded in John 12 the disciples raised their voices and thought it a waste. Why not rather have sold the ointment and given the money to the poor, they objected.

I personally know very talented and gifted Christians (in reality we all are very talented and gifted) who are either unemployed or just are home and thus from a human perspective seemingly are wasting their lives. Their surroundings might be accusing them of laziness or listlessness. In addition to being subject to those well meaning person's ideas of a productive life many of them also have to struggle with condemnation or sentiments that are challenging their self-esteem because they somehow seems out of the loop.

This idea of waste also comes into play in regard to ministry. Large parts of Christianity have some preconceived notions when it comes to ministry and how we are to serve in a church or a denomination. When we for some reason fall outside these confines we are regarded as wasting our talents or something in that direction. The main goal in most Christianity is to see people saved. That is a noble goal. However, we have too long seen this as an ordinance and not a promise.

Mary's offer drew attention to Christ. You have given yourself to Christ as a fragrant ointment, and by that offer you are drawing people to Christ often without you being consciously aware of this most wonderful and astounding fact. That is how a supernatural promise plays out. While you are resting in Him with your unique personality He makes Himself known to the world through you. It isn't something you can control. He does it perfectly both through your negatives and your positives.

My friend, when you have come to Christ nothing in your life is a waste. Everything you do, don't do or are is an expensive ointment in God's eyes. You are a blessing to Him regardless of your circumstances. Don't listen to those who say your life would be more of a blessing if you just would give yourself to the poor, that is, whatever cause they find worthy or imagine need your support.

The Spirit is a Rebel

When the Spirit has led you through the wilderness and conditioned you through that experience so that you are receptive for the revelations which follow and which will cause an end to your self-efforts and establish you in the union with God, He will keenly guard your new standing in Christ. Every time someone attempts to subject you to laws, that is, outer ordinances such as should, ought to, should not etc you will sense something rise within you. The sensation can most closely be likened to defiance. In the beginning we are perhaps too well behaved to let the Rebel have His way. However, as He trains us we begin to recognize this rebellious sensation as Him. As an effect we adamantly refuse to let anyone rob from us our freedom in Christ regardless of who that tries to impose their moralistic outlook upon us. The Spirit is the Spirit of truth and freedom, and He lives within every believer making sure that we become rebels as well, insurrectionists that shake the religious world.

The Treasure

"But we have this treasure in earthen vessels, that the excellency of the power may be of God, and not of us. ... that the life also of Jesus might be made manifest in our body, ... that the life also of Jesus might be made manifest in our mortal flesh." (2 Cor. 4:7,10,11)

The new creation is filled with a treasure which is active and divine in its nature. Since its principal characteristic is love this presence flows through the new man with a power which overcomes death and guarantees an overflow of life in the vessel. A torrent is created that will make its influence known in everything in its vicinity. Those who are midst in this river of life know that the power is not of themselves. Every desire of imitation is quenched when the living water manifests its invisibility in human flesh. Garden life is again restored in its simplicity and perfection in a beloved creature who finds that this is the eternity embedded in its heart. Christ as us is a blossoming flowerbed of diversity. The inner law of life far surpasses any outer law of death. Human notions such as motivation and examples, which stir the flesh, are declared obsolete when the real thing manifests itself – the very manifestation of Christ in us as us.

Bond Servants

There are depths to the Genesis account which are quite amazing. Sometimes it seems as there are layers like a onion which the Spirit peels away as He finds edifying. Some are given to see this and others are given to see that. One fascinating aspect that I have been allowed to ponder lately is seeing Eve as a type of the human race and Adam as a type of Christ. Adam is in a odd way both a type of Christ and not a type of Christ. In one sentence he is and in the next he is not. When he is not he is merely that old Adam who seemingly messed everything up. We like to think that he is at fault. In a way he is, but from a different perspective without his disobedience we still would have been children spiritually speaking. I think his fall was inevitable in order to bring forth a succession of sons who are conscious of all aspects of life.

Let us first examine Eve as a type of the human race and Adam as a type of Christ. We notice that Eve was the first to eat of the forbidden tree. Adam was by her side all along. Due to his love towards her and that he couldn't stand the thought of losing her he also partook of the tree. That was the only way that Jesus could save us. He had to become a man and partake in our world. More than that; he had to taste the death that were our destiny. So Adam eating of the forbidden fruit in a way foreshadows Jesus atoning death on our behalf. Jesus and the Father love us so highly that Jesus has stood by our side all along. He has been so unwilling to lose us that He was willing to taste the same fruit as we all taste; death. The sting of sin is death, and Jesus became sin for us.

Genesis 3:16 states that our desire shall be for our husband. Here we are Eve again, the woman who becomes pregnant with the children of her husband. The record further says that in pain we shall bring forth our children when our husband is that old Adam. His seed in us causes us to struggle in pain when we attempt to do right. We find that we fail miserably and the consequence is a soul wrenching condemnation. It should be quite clear thus that when we die from our husband and is free to marry another we are redeemed from that former curse, and childbearing becomes a restful expression of our new husband, which is Christ.

If we despite this continue to struggle after our marriage with Christ it merely is an indication of us being taken through the wilderness until that illusion about separation is done away with. We became one with Christ the day we accepted Him, but somehow our minds haven't quite grasped this tremendous fact so we continue to struggle erroneously thinking that being a bond-servant of Christ is based on the same terms as when we were bond-servants under our old master. Being a bond-servant of Christ denotes an absolutely different quality of life compared to the life under that old Adam. Christ's will is our will. His abundant life is our abundant life. His freedom is our freedom. More than that; since there is no separation we are

Him in our form, each of us expressing Him in our uniqueness so that the total becomes His body in this world.

As unredeemed men and women we didn't know that we were someone's spouses or bond-servants. We thought we were free agents operating as independent units. It isn't until the Spirit opens our inner eyes that we become aware of our true standing, and we for the first time begin to see how things really are. Paradoxically, that is a part of the liberation process towards maturity and inner peace. You see, God has been with you all along. He has never turned His glance away from you. He loves you so intensely that He has completely identified with your falls and failures so that you could come out, of what has seemed like a mess to you, like a whole person knowing beyond a shadow of doubt that He is fond of you, and that you are His beloved child. He has never turned His back on you. You might have thought or felt that He wasn't there when things were dark. But, there He was all along partaking in your unique life with everything He is; Himself.

Comfort for Broken Hearts

When God is pursuing you with His love He never asks those tricky and humiliating questions regarding your past such as; How did this happen? Why did you do that? Why on earth would you do such a thing? Rather, He asks those questions which sole purpose are to make you feel comfortable in His presence. They often go like this: How are you? How's your day been? Can I help you in any way? You know that I love you? We are talking about those questions which make you feel at ease and which convey His unconditional love towards you. Unconditional love is concerned with you and your heart's condition.

God's main business is those inward things. He wants to heal your heart, your inner man. That is the place where those most hurting wounds are; the pain or fear or insecurity which in a way renders you as a crippling emotionally speaking. A healed and redeemed heart is the greatest miracle there is. We know from the scriptures that Jesus had a magnificent healing ministry. He often healed all those who came to Him. Those miracles as they are recorded in the gospels deal mainly with the outer man, that is, bodily ailments. We construe those incidents accordingly, and thus when we read that Jesus promised that we would do greater miracles than Him we begin to pray for those who are sick. Unfortunately, our most frequent experience is that nothing happens and we thus easily become disillusioned.

Why does the gospels seemingly merely record outer healings? Isn't it because those miracles get our attention? They create a desire in us to deliver people from their ailments. And it is easier to depict the effects of an outer healing than an inner healing. An objective reality is much more convenient to describe than the subjective surrealism of a complex inner world. As we mature we grow from outer perception to inner perception and we begin to appreciate that in reality everything is about that inner world. Our bodies are merely our temporarily abodes which are predestined to decay as we are waiting for our final liberation. Our heart, however, is eternal. When we move from outer to inner we rapidly acknowledge that we do greater miracles than Jesus since His love in us ministers love and healing to others in a grand scale.

There is no doubt in my mind that God in His grace still delivers people from diseases and ailments. However, we also find ample evidence that good people die from for instance cancer far too early despite the fact that they are subject to intense prayer. However, it seems as the spiritual law which states that when the seed falls into the ground and die this single seed gives life to many is still very potent. Jesus was a prime example regarding the effects of this law. The literature is also full of examples which confirm that God is greater than our afflictions and can turn everything into something good for many. "The tortures occur", CS Lewis wrote, "If they are unnecessary, then there is no God, or a bad one. If there is a good God, then these tortures are necessary for no even moderately good Being could possibly inflict or permit them if they weren't"

His Truth

Gideon was beating out wheat in the wine press terrified by the Midian oppressors when God spoke His word of faith over him: "The Lord is with you, O mighty man of valour." As most of us Gideon was fixed on circumstances and appearances, and found it quite impossible to reconcile what he so clearly saw in the temporal realm with what God saw in the spiritual dimension. Gideon thus echoed a common theme in his reply: "My clan is the weakest one, and I am the least of them all."

God calls into existence the things that do not exist. In Gideon's case God didn't appreciate the lie about Gideon which Gideon held fast to in the midst of his travails. From his viewpoint Gideon couldn't see any further than the lie. When God has spoken His truth about a person or a situation His truth will come to pass despite every circumstance. So, Gideon became ultimately in the natural what God already saw in faith.

As new creations we are faith people. God's intention with every one of us is to transform our entire outlook so that we can behold everything through faith. It is by faith that His love and generosity become manifest to us. It is by faith we understand that His desires are our desires. It is by faith we with firm boldness can speak to things which do not exist as they exist, because they do in the eternal realm. We might perhaps not see them come to pass in our lifetime, but ultimately they will become a reality.

We all experience situations which seem to overwhelm us, which we have no clue how to handle with our limited human means. We often encounter this devastating sensation of being nothing. In the natural we see our heritage, our humanity, the city we are from and our family line. We hear the mocking voice in our head asserting all the lies about our person which are so easy to believe, because the natural seemingly confirms his accusations. Then God speaks His truth unto us, and everything is turned upside down. And He persistently pursues His truth until it is established as a fact in our minds.

Twelve years ago I sat in church feeling as a complete failure as a father. Then this voice interrupted my outpouring and plainly stated which such an authority that my world was turned completely around: "To your children you are the best dad in the world."

The Junction

One day we come to a junction in our lives. We are purposely led there by the Spirit. The issue we are confronted with is a faith issue. The Bible says that there is no condemnation for those who are in Christ Jesus. It asserts that there is a rest for God's people where they rest from their own works. John even states that a person born of God cannot sin. However, we are daily perplexed by life in the sense that we experience condemnation, we struggle to please God and we try to avoid committing sins. It becomes quite clear to us that our experiences contradict the scriptures. When that is the case there obviously must be something missing in our understanding. We have reached the junction.

The Spirit has caught us in a dilemma, and He states that there is only one solution; we have to make a leap of faith into the mystery. Paul writes that there is a mystery which has been hidden from ages and generations, but now is revealed to the saints; Christ in you. He writes to the Galatians that it pleased God to reveal His Son in Paul. He continues to say that Christ lives in Him, and he even states that when the churches of Judea heard that he who once persecuted the church now preached the faith they glorified God in Paul. He says that the gospel he preaches is not man's gospel. There obviously is a man's gospel which is contrary to the gospel Paul preached. So before we make the leap and enter into the mystery we obviously have been under influence of man's gospel. A gospel that causes confusion and is accursed since it keeps the saints in bondage.

It begins to dawn upon us that if all the above mentioned is the case then we must somehow be Christ in our form, that we are partakers of divine nature. This is the secret, the solution to our predicament. Completely taken over by God we are new creations, and we begin to see that our main problem has been those thought patterns that have insisted that there is a separation between us and God; He there and me over here. However, if we are one spirit with Him there is no separation and we are rightly gods. Our rest means that we have entered the seventh day; the day when the heavens and the earth were finished, and all the host of them. United with God and settled with Him on the seventh day we are complete and perfected once and for all, simply because all is finished. When we have a consciousness of sin our mindset is separation and we believe that we live in one of the other six days of work. If we believe so we obviously believe in an illusion, because He has finished the work. There is nothing we can add.

Remember that when you accepted Christ you were firmly placed on the seventh day with God, resting from all your works. Our main problem is that we haven't discovered this actuality yet. So in reality we struggle in vain when we think we aren't placed there. Remember, we cannot add a single thing to His work. All our efforts are therefore just wind.

At the junction the Spirit urges us to make that leap of faith which settles us on the seventh day in our consciousnesses, where we align faith with facts.

Walk on Waters

When Jesus walked on the water it was not only a demonstration that God is above and can operate outside the physical laws. It is a statement that God is far greater than any physical law. But, as with most stories in the Bible there is much more to this incident than what meets the eye. God is spirit and manifests Himself in the natural, and thus when the Spirit utilizes figures in the natural to prove a point there is irrevocably a spiritual dimension to this that only can be appreciated through revelation.

When Jesus annuls the physical laws by walking on the water He also states that He is above the moral laws as recorded in the commandments. In Him they are canceled and He is above and outside their domain. Thus He is a law in Himself, spontaneously expressing God, who is love, in His physical body. He is like the wind that blows wherever it pleases. It is constrained by nothing, and blows in every direction the Spirit instigates always confusing and confounding those who live by appearances like Peter when he couldn't fathom and resisted that Jesus had to die at the cross.

Walking on the water Jesus beckons and calls every one of us to join Him. The power of the outer laws is indeed so authoritative that it is only when we are in Him that we are out of their insisting reach. In Him we are set free from any law that is operative in the natural realm. Immediately we fix the gaze at ourselves and our own abilities we begin to sink. As the water begins to envelope us and we can sense how it presses in from every direction we are again subject to the all the laws which threaten to drag us down into the black abyss of captivity and death.

We have now tasted both; captivity and liberty, and as Peter we prefer the sensation of being unlimited. Therefore in our distress we call out for Jesus. The Spirit has taken us through both these extremes to teach us the wonders of the heavenly life and that it is not in our powers to sustain this life. It is only attainable in our union with Christ where we rest from our own abilities after the Spirit has taught us the futility of trusting our own efforts.

Many of us have had those dreams where we are freed from the natural laws and fly through the air in amazed wonder. Deep down in every one of us there is a yearning to experience the supernatural, freed from every inhibiting circumstance. In Christ we begin to manifest our dream. When we recognize that we are in Him everything is now possible. We can do nothing of ourselves, but in Him we are far above the limitations of human law. In Him weakness is turned into strength. Span your wings and fly, says the Spirit.

The Damascus Road

There on the road to Damascus Saul met the resurrected Christ. He had heard about Jesus and His earthly service. As most Pharisees He believed Jesus was an imposter. Vehemently Saul persecuted those following the way. Even though Saul most likely hadn't met Jesus he knew him according to the flesh. How he perceived Jesus and His ministry was merely one-dimensional, and Saul hadn't much regard for this in many ways ordinary person's claims of being the savior of the world.

The only way to know the resurrected Christ is by becoming blind to knowing Jesus only after the flesh. Blind to the earthly realities Saul's inner eyes were opened to grasp the enormity of the cross. In his blindness he could acquaint the invisible Christ. The Saul whose whole life had been engrossed in the outer things became Paul who led a life from inner realities. Fixed in the inner realities of the spiritual world he regained his vision so that he could influence the outer world.

The loss of sight also denotes our utter helplessness in our encounter with Christ. We have nothing to offer except our lives through which He can reach out to a world that believe it is seeing, but is truly blind. Until we have become blind to the outer world we have no proper vision. It is when we become blind that we become seers. As seers we recognize our nothingness and His superior abilities to live the life we all are created to be partakers of.

At the Damascus road we all get our new name. The name that has been a part of our self consciousness to this point is declared void and of no effect when we meet Christ. Our new name comes into effect when we are baptized into Christ. It severed our strings to the past and all those old lies which have kept us in bondage and without hope in this world. It denotes a completely new direction, and it accentuates our new standing as new creations with hope for the future.

When Saul encountered Jesus a light from heaven flashed around him. The Spirit opens our eyes so that we are enabled to see Jesus in a new light.

Seeing Jesus merely after the flesh causes us to want to emulate His deeds and attitudes without acknowledging the Spirit dimension of His life. He is both flesh and spirit, and so are we; flesh made perfect by the Spirit. Flesh is spirit manifested and that is our glory.

We are Both – That is our Glory

Legalism is a system of living whereby we try to make spiritual progress or gain by following a system of rules or ordinances. The fundamental idea is to try to make ourselves presentable to God by doing right. We find this concept in all religions, Christianity is no exception. Paul said in one of his epistles that we no longer know Jesus after the flesh. This is the antidote to legalism. When we know a so called spiritual leader merely after the flesh we immediately begin to wish to emulate that person's behavior, thinking and attitudes. This is the principal motivation behind legalism; man imitating man, or man attempting to please a distant God.

The other extreme is those spiritual systems which emphasize the spiritual dimension only. One of their favorite assertions is that the material world merely is an illusion, that the only reality is the spiritual. Today's New Age movement in many ways belongs to this branch of the religious world. However, if we are to find the right balance we cannot exclude the flesh, that is, our soul and bodies. Jesus came in the flesh as a real person. We thus cannot ditch our own flesh. Fred Pruitt puts it like this: "He was flesh and blood real, which is why it is the real and actual sacrifice of His Body and His shed blood can be efficacious in our lives. We can know our humanity filled with God and doing His will by us, only because we have been shown another humanity which was/is just the same. We MUST keep the human side, and not toss it out in favor of a Spirit-side only."

John writes in the first chapter of his gospel: "And the Word was made flesh, and dwelt among us, (and we beheld his glory, the glory as of the only begotten of the Father,) full of grace and truth." It was spirit manifested in flesh that enabled the disciples to behold Jesus' glory. As

126

sons of the Most High we are also spirits manifested in flesh, and that is our glory. If we exclude any of those attributes we have left true Christianity and are an easy prey to aberrations. The Spirit was the basis of Jesus' life, works, thoughts and attitudes. That was His rest and that is our rest. A Spirit led life isn't about imitation, because "the wind blows wherever it pleases. You hear its sound, but you cannot tell where it comes from or where it is going. So it is with everyone born of the Spirit." The Spirit-flesh dimension encourages us to acknowledge that life is about diversity, different gifts and personalities, different paths and uniqueness.

To know Jesus no longer after the flesh is to recognize that there was/is an additional dimension to His life which we also are partakers of. Fred Pruitt writes: "Jesus only walked out as a parable what was already true in the Spirit, from the way and manner in which He lived and walked, to the Cross which is a real space-time event on earth, but which cut across all divisions between time and eternity and bridged the gap. We must have them both, not one or the other. We live in time and eternity, and in Christ become "masters" of both. Boehme said we have in a sense two eyes, one which sees forward into eternity, and the other which sees backward into time. One who has overcome will understand this and live it."

The resurrected Christ manifested Himself to the disciples and Thomas in particular. Jesus was so real in the flesh that he challenged Thomas to put his hand into His side. He showed Thomas His hands. Jesus said: "Stop doubting and believe!" Then Thomas exclaimed:"My Lord and my God!"

His Second Coming

This is how Lucas depicts Jesus' ascension: "And while they looked stedfastly toward heaven as he went up, behold, two men stood by them in white apparel; Which also said, Ye men of Galilee, why stand ye gazing up into heaven? this same Jesus, which is taken up from you into heaven, shall so come in like manner as ye have seen him go into heaven. (Acts 1:10-11)"

In John chapter 16 Jesus tells the disciples, "in a little while you will see me no more, and then after a little while you will see me." When Jesus used the phrase "in a little while" He obviously meant a period of days. We know that is a fact regarding His ascension. Since He uses the same phrase about His return He meant that after a period of days they would see Him again.

In the last chapter of his Gospel John writes that Jesus showed Himself three times to the disciples after His resurrection. It wasn't a ghost they saw but a real person in flesh and blood as witnessed in particular by Thomas when he was offered to put his hand into Jesus' side.

When the two men in white said that Jesus would come back in the same way as the disciples had seen Him go into heaven they meant that Jesus would return in flesh. He had ascended in the flesh and He would return in the flesh. The Jews are still waiting for their Messiah. They missed His coming, and are thus still waiting. Large parts of Christianity are still waiting for Jesus' second coming. As the Jews they have missed the event, because Jesus has indeed returned in the flesh after a little while as He promised.

The Jews missed Jesus because they couldn't fathom that He would be born as a poor unnoticed child in a manger. They thought He would come with flashing lights, great pageantry and ethereal splendor. Christianity has missed Jesus second coming because they cannot fathom that He has returned as you and me who are quite ordinary persons in the flesh. We are that manger where Jesus is born again and again. Paul puts it like this: "To them God has chosen to make known among the Gentiles the glorious riches of this mystery, which is Christ in you, the hope of glory."

In the book of revelation John writes: "Behold, he is coming with the clouds, and every eye will see him." In the literature we find a myriad of imaginative attempts at explaining this verse. Notably that all will see Him has puzzled many a commentator. However, if Jesus has returned in a host of born again Christians this passage suddenly makes a lot of sense.

There are passages in the Bible which allude to that there will be an additional second coming beyond the one discussed in this brief article. However, this particular event is hidden from me, so all I can say is: time will show.

Love Your Neighbor As Yourself

Love your neighbor as yourself, has been one of those major stumbling blocks in my life. I knew what the commandment demanded from me, but I was utterly helpless in fulfilling it. One day I saw that it said that I couldn't love my neighbor more than I could love myself. A life in condemnation and failure isn't of much help if you are to love yourself. This whole scheme seemed more like an endless loop of misery than something that was possible to attain. I guess this was how the Israelites felt when they wandered in circles in the wilderness.

Love your neighbor as yourself is in fact a double commandment where love your neighbor hinges on love yourself. Self love and self acceptance is a prerequisite for the other. If we view this commandment from an outer perspective it soon becomes a burden to big for us to carry on our shoulders. The secret of fulfilling of Jesus' seemingly impossible demand is found on a completely different level.

We read that Jesus was perfected through what He suffered. The ultimate goal of everything God does is to make sure that Christ is formed in us, so that we can be transformed to His image. This implies a process where we ultimately come to the end of ourselves and appreciate our nothingness, where we as Jesus say that we can do nothing of ourselves. We kick out, or more precisely; in a joint operation with the Spirit we kick out, any residues of self-reliance and any desires to make things happen of our own accord. We arrive at the spot where we become still and acknowledge that God is God. That illusion of independent self is once and for all shattered.

Abraham was also perfected through what he suffered. Of old age, when his loins were empty, when he had encountered his own nothingness God could plant the seed in Sara which brought forth Isaac, who was a fruit of the Spirit with eternal repercussions. From his line Jesus was born. However, the seed could not be planted before Abraham's nothingness was amalgamated with faith. Through what he suffered Abraham was empowered to see beyond himself and see God only, as the one who would and could accomplish His will in and through Abraham.

When Abraham initially saw his nothingness and coupled it with what God had promised him he bordered on the verge of bitterness and cynicism. God, however, continued to remind Abraham about His promise and thus slowly but surely fuelled Abraham's faith until Abraham recognized that in his nothingness was the seed to supernatural greatness in God. In his nothingness he found his true life, the abundant life of faith.

We all receive the same invitation as Abraham, to leave everything behind and find a place where we can set up our tent and be met by our God who through our nothingness can conceive the boy, that is, the righteous deeds that are everlasting in their effect. Like Abraham we are not guaranteed in our lifetime to see the multitude of seeds from the one seed.

As Lot we all ran when it began to rain sulfur and fire upon us. From the horizon we could behold the smoking ruins of our self righteous works or attempts thereof. Free from any obligations to perform, reliant on God only we have discovered our nothingness. In this nothingness we are wholly His responsibility and we say as Jesus: I only do what I see my Father is doing. We even say as Paul: By His grace I am what I am. The nothingness is our freedom. No need to pretend anymore. When it now dawns upon me that I am accepted and loved by God as His unique creation I can love myself without reservation and from the new heart flows love to my neighbor in the manner God see most fit for my neighbor's eternal destiny.

Kissed on the Inside

We have all wondered about what the difference is between human love and God's love. The scriptures tell us that God is love. It isn't something He has. It is something He is. That simple fact transcends our understanding. What many of us try to do in order to understand God's quality of love is that we attempt to explain it with human words and definitions. However, the Bible says that the world is deceived by the evil one so our ideas of love will be heavy influenced with his ideas of love, which really isn't love.

The plain fact is that humans love from the outside. This is demonstrated by how we kiss the outside, and we all know what feelings and sensations that arouses. God, however, kisses the inside. We only know a person from the outside. The outside is what we see and perceive regarding a person. In addition we perhaps know something about a person from what she or he has told us. We have a very limited knowledge about what stirs a person and the inner processes that shape that person's conduct and outlook.

God knows all those things. He knows the depths of our being. Our history is intimately known by Him. He knows perfectly well what stirs and motivates us. The patterns of behavior and thinking that make a person are all familiar to Him. We would easily be tempted to say that He loves us despite all His encompassing knowledge about us. It is so convenient to disparage our worth and our being when we marvel at His love. The truth is that we are created in His likeness. Thus we have the potential to understand His love. Moreover, we have the potential to love like He does.

Jesus was an example of us, that is, what is possible when flesh and Spirit is intertwined in a union where oneness with God is an established reality. To love like God is not a self improvement program, but life that flows from a person that is indwelled by God. If God is love so are we. Only faith can appropriate this amazing wonder.

To be kissed on the inside is such a new and unfortunately alien experience for us that it takes a huge job from the Spirit to convince us about what God is doing in our lives. He kisses our history, our thinking, our incentives, our inner person, yes, everything that we are. It is a perpetual love feast. His kisses find all those spots that hurt and confuse us. His kisses untangle those knots that make us cringe in fear and despair. Even when all those deceptions which have kept us in bondage all our lives are stamped out He continues to kiss us.

In the Beginning

In front of Pilate Jesus said that His kingdom wasn't of this world. This is a kingdom which government is found inside humans created in the likeness of God. In order to understand this kingdom we have to return to the beginning where everything was void and silent. The Spirit is hovering over this nothingness which we all have to return to or be led back to before His creative forces can be unleashed in us.

Our return to the beginning is marked by frustrations, sufferings and failures. That is the only way our self activity and noise can be extinguished. We all initially thought that Christianity was all about moving fast towards some goal God had set up for us. The faster we got there the better Christians we were, and the more God would be pleased with us. We thought it was about becoming something or someone. That is was about doing the right things, having the right motivation, the right attitude. We thought we should imitate Jesus. We spoke a lot about love, but couldn't quite find it within ourselves.

However, Christianity is about moving slowly to the beginning where we ultimately recognize our nothingness and become still. In the stillness God is moving, and we in this stillness recognize His mighty power within which created the heavens and earth. It dawns upon us that there is no separation between us and Him. He is in us presenting Himself to the world through each unique seed.

We all have the capacity for thinking, and we have a consciousness. To us it seems like our mental activity takes place somewhere on the inside of our bodies. However, we cannot pinpoint its exact location. It seems, though, as it is confined inside our flesh. But, what if we didn't have any flesh? Where would our thinking and consciousness be then? It would just float unimpeded in the void. This is the place where we are linked to God, who is all in all, and who in His great wisdom decided to contain His all-ness or omnipresence in humans like you and me. When we return to the beginning, to the void, to our nothingness we find God and His kingdom within and all is well.

No Wrath

Before we have been led by the Spirit backwards to the void we still have residues of separation in our mindsets and this illusion generates another illusion regarding God's wrath. We repeatedly find this theme in the old testament when an unredeemed people fears God's wrath at every corner. From Adam's fall and onward separation from God was how the chosen people viewed their existence, and as a consequence they dreaded God and His wrath.

When we as mature people recognize our nothingness we find that our lives have been hidden in Christ all along, and there in the void we find our lives again in Him as an everlasting outflow of light. More than that, we discover that the idea about God's wrath was another of those tricks of the enemy, but which the Spirit has used with great efficiency so that we can come to end of ourselves. The Spirit has led us backward to our origin where we find no wrath. When the illusion about separation evaporates the illusion about God's wrath is made void and nothing.

We have come to the point which the scriptures call before the foundation of the earth. At this point the lamb was slain and God wrath evaporated. To us this point in time is now. Every now is thus before the foundation of the earth. In the temporal realm the cross is the focal point which stretches both backward and forward in time. Before the foundation of the earth can't be expressed with words or understood in terms of time. It is in the same manner as He is, the great I AM, and we are in the eternal. Eternally bound to Him in love and a part of Him we find that our wrath was an illusion as well. The eternal outpouring of light and love is the sole and only reality. Finally we know what Jesus meant when He spoke about a peace that transcends understanding.

We Are the Light of the World

There is an eternal outflow of light from God. It expels darkness wherever its rays penetrate. Every man who is joined one Spirit with the Father through the redemption in Jesus Christ is also an eternal outflow of light. In our ignorance we thought that we had to become light, to let our light shine brighter and more radiantly through a change of behavior. In Christ we are the light of the world and we are placed on a hill so that our light is seen by all who have eyes to see.

The question about sin always raises its ugly head in this context. Won't sin extinguish our light? That is a question children in Christ ask, and the answer we give them is no! An adult in Christ has no consciousness of sin because he not only believe, but knows, that a once and for all sacrifice for sin has made the sin issue void and of no interest. His only concern is life in its many facets. Thus, he like Jesus exerts his right to forgive anyone his sin. Our mission is reconciliation and not sin. The light in us compels us to implore people on Christ's behalf to be reconciled with God.

But, don't we have flaws and shortcomings that obstruct the light? No! Those are the cracks in the jar which the light finds its way through. If God has declared us perfect in His Son, then we are perfect. As adults we have advanced past that level where we were preoccupied with our flaws. We have put that change me, do me better attitude behind us. It isn't about us anymore, but Christ and those He loves. The light in us finds those He has given us. They are caught in our spotlight, and the darkness in and around them is expelled by the heavenly rays. We see this happen by our inner eye, that is, faith!

In the Cool of the Day

God walked among Eve and Adam in the midst of the garden in the cool of the day. His presence wasn't unassuming, but it wasn't threatening or obtrusive in any way. It was more like a pleasant breeze that cools you down after a warm and strenuous day. Eve and Adam didn't know what shame was, so despite their nakedness they were attracted to this amiable and loving presence with whom they could share they hearts.

The Fall changed everything. It wasn't God that changed. It was man. Man's nakedness suddenly became a distress and an annoyance in his own eyes. He was so bothered by the fact that he hadn't anything to offer God that that crippling sensation of shame completely prostrated him. Even worse, he felt so devastatingly unclean compared to the radiant holiness of God. Shame efficiently put up a barrier where before there had been a silent torrent of love flowing between the two lovers. Shame made man hide from God, and wherever there is shame man hides from the only source which can remove shame.

Ever since that day there has been a burning desire in God's heart to see the intimacy of the Garden restored. In Christ the objective was achieved. In Christ there is no shame. As we move further and further into this mystery of Him being in us and we in Him we find our nakedness again. Nakedness in Him connotes that our original potential is restored to express Him as sons and daughters, as His beloved heirs in a world that is craving for redemption.

When the relationship is restored God walks in the midst of our lives like a cool breeze which gingerly caress our cheeks with affection and love. As the Spirit removes those last residues of shame in our outlook and the last clouds, which have obstructed our vision, evaporate we see that we are perpetually intertwined with Him and that we are the Garden which now blossoms with a lush exuberance that is spectacular in its radiance and beauty.

Made in the USA
Lexington, KY
12 April 2015